Blogging Made Easy

By
Amen Sharma, Gareth James, Romeo Martin J. Rosales and Rumena Begum

Hashtagblogger.com
RumenaBegum.com

Special Thanks To:

Katie Corio, Katie Hall, Kavita Sharma, Paz Sharma, Samad Khan and Sophie Charlton.

Table of Contents

Introduction

We here at Hashtag Blogger have teamed up with internet sensation Rumena Begum to provide you with 'Blogging Made Easy'.

We have written the guides in this book to help you make the most out of life as a blogger in 2016 and help you take your success to the next level by attracting more visitors and increasing your online exposure.

Whether you're starting up a new blog, have done blogging for years, or you're running a blog for your business. We're going to cover everything you need to know in order to have a successful online blog. We'll also explain how you can outreach and get noticed by brands looking for collaborations.

Technical Skills & Requirements

Most of the guides provided in our book are easy enough to execute with minimal technical skill. We recommend you go over our guides and allocate as much as you can to your team and if you struggle with the more technical guides give your web developer a call or speak to us for help.

A Free Gift For Our Readers

As a thank you for purchasing this book and to give you a head start with your blog and online marketing, we would like to offer you a very special free gift.

We're offering our readers a 3-day free Instagram engagement campaign.

Instagram engagement campaigns are used by all the top bloggers you see trending every day. These campaigns are used to help seek the attention of brands looking for bloggers to represent their products and at times even be paid for a review.

To claim your free Instagram engagement offer visit; http://www.hashtagblogger.com/instagram-engagement-campaign/

You can also visit our website and click the offers tab to claim this offer.

About Rumena Begum

My name is Rumena Begum I am a 23-year-old Bangladeshi fashion & beauty blogger based in London. I grew up with 6 amazing sisters who are my best friends; I am third in line in case you're wondering. I have lived in London my whole life and just recently started taking blogging seriously but never did I ever imagine it would one day turn into my full-time job. If you'd like to learn more about me please continue reading. Firstly, I had no intention of becoming a blogger it was coincidental.

I was academically bright, I achieved 9 out of 10 GCSE grades then went onto to study further at college. I studied Law, English, Psychology and Sociology, however, I dropped English in my second year. I really enjoyed my two years at college; I became so passionate about Law I decided I wanted to continue studying Law at University. I went to the University of Westminster and didn't really enjoy studying Law or studying in general. I found myself getting very bored and I lost interest, studies was not doing any justice for me, I took a turn for the better and dropped out of University because fashion and beauty were my aspirations! Dropping out of uni was one of the best decisions I've ever made in life.

I worked in retail for a good year trying to save money for a makeup course, which was really expensive! I wanted to achieve a qualification on makeup to give me a head start in the beauty industry. After I completed a 5-day intensive makeup course with Lubna Rafiq I used my Instagram to promote myself and build my clientele. At that point, I already had a fairly big following of about 10,000 followers on Instagram and I took full advantage of this and began to promote my work. The more engagement there is on your page the better. It shows you are active and you're taking your job seriously.

I received a tonne of bookings and I grew a passion for makeup. I was finally doing something I really enjoyed and I was earning at the same time. A couple months down the line my Instagram started kicking off, not only did I upload makeup related posts but I also uploaded images of me wearing different western/eastern outfits that drew more attention to my page. I received so much love and positivity on my Instagram page it was unreal. The more posts I uploaded the more active my Instagram was. My Instagram is open to the public so anyone who came across my page would be able to see my posts and follow if they genuinely took an interest in what I do! I never privatised my account, as a private account would be pointless for a blogger. If you really want to get yourself out there you must allow everyone to stumble across your social media platforms, if they like what they see they will follow you anyway.

I started blogging/YouTube only because I received a tonne of requests to do so. People loved what they saw and wanted me to take it further. I was a bit reluctant at first, I doubted myself because I didn't think I'd be able to do it however I listened to my followers and gave it a shot, no harm in trying best thing I've ever done. I was so eager to make this work when I started up my YouTube channel I invested a lot of money into equipment as I wanted to upload good quality videos, I was not great at first as I always had issues with lighting, however, I took into account my followers feedback and always made improvements based on their feedback. Every time I created content for my YouTube channel and received positive feedback it only motivated me to upload more often and make it a full-time thing. My following grew rapidly and I was getting noticed by companies/brands. The first step to success is to be true to yourself then true to everyone else, I have full control over everything I do I decide the companies I want to work with, I don't just promote everything and anything because if I did then no one would take me seriously. Never falsely advertise in exchange for money be real, be open and you'd gain a lot more respect and a lot more recognition.

I still haven't fulfilled half of my dreams but that's ok because I'm trying and that's enough. Don't expect things to happen overnight being a successful blogger takes time, effort and determination. If you're willing to work hard then just know it'll definitely pay off and it will be worth it in the end. I used to do a lot of work for free just to grow my platform, to get recognised and to become successful. I started earning from blogging only when I knew my platform became influential, beneficial and made a difference to a lot of people, companies and brands. Another thing I did to get myself out there was attend big and small events. At events, you will meet a variety of different people from different backgrounds, occupations etc. I found it very beneficial for me as It was a chance to network with people and give them an insight of what I do. Word of mouth is very effective the more people that know of you the better for you, whether it's good or bad you're still a topic they're discussing. Try and attend as many events as you can you'll always meet someone new that didn't know about you.

Get yourself on different social media platforms the more platforms you promote yourself on the more recognition you'll receive, for example, there might be someone on Twitter who doesn't follow you on Instagram. There will be a different following and engagement on each platform which is always good! I am absolutely obsessed with Snapchat because for me it's like daily vlogging I get to interact with my followers so well, it has definitely made a difference. On Snapchat once a week (sometimes more) I do a Snapchat update now this is a life update about myself and what I have been up to, I really get to express my thoughts, feelings and share my experiences, that's what people love seeing because they can really see the person I am. I receive so many messages to do a Snapchat update, people enjoy watching me and usually, I'll always have a positive message to deliver. People often forget that Bloggers are normal people just like everyone else only difference is we decide to broadcast everything.

Becoming a successful blogger will not be a smooth ride expect the good and bad that comes with it. Always be well organised and think one step ahead, having a structured plan on what you intend to deliver is a good start. Find out what you're good at and what you're passionate about and focus on that. If you're truly passionate about something others will see that and appreciate it. Sometimes you have to make tiny sacrifices but that should only motivate you to do better. Think outside the box, think positive, make things happen and start today!

Why This Book

Bloggers are seen as a highly influential crowd, bloggers are early adopters, having embraced new trends far more quickly than ever before. Individuals use blogging, vlogs (video blogging) and social media to make a name for themselves, establish a personal brand and become an influencer in their niche. 81% of the population trusts the advice they get from bloggers, making bloggers very powerful advocates for any brand or business. Brands are looking for bloggers to work with everyday and we've decided to help and educate the average blogger to become the next Zoella (www.instagram.com/zoella/).

The new generation of online shoppers, spend more time watching videos on YouTube than they do watching TV, and much prefer to watch YouTubers to get ideas and watch reviews before purchasing products. Bloggers such as Zoella are now household names thanks to Instagram and she is banking approximately £50k a month.

Zoella made her fame by reviewing everyday beauty and fashion products on her website and social media channels. Soon after Google indexed her pages for keywords such as 'makeup reviews' and her website traffic went from hundreds to millions of views overnight.

That's why we've written this book, because every day we'll receive hundreds of direct messages on Instagram from bloggers wanting a shoutout, more exposure and help with their blog sites.

Rumena's Case Study

I never thought that having my own website would make a difference. I'm always so busy with Instagram, Snapchat and YouTube that I never really worried about having a website.

I've always wanted to work with Sigma Beauty, and I've emailed them so many times asking if I can review their products. They always replied with 'unfortunately at this time.....'.

Surprisingly the day my website went live, I got the following e-mail;

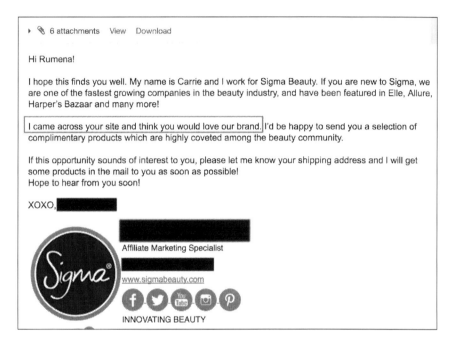

This email was literally sent to me within 24 hours of my website going live and I was so happy to know the impact it makes to have a Google friendly blog site.

Katie Corio's Case Study

Social media has redefined what it takes to be successful. Within less than one year, my life has turned into more than I could ever have imagined possible—and it is all due to hard work, passion, a little luck and social media.

My name is Katie Corio, I am a 23-year-old living in San Diego, CA. I run an online coaching business for personal training and nutrition, as well as work as an independent contractor for two major companies in the fitness industry.

My total projected income for this year is going to be well over six figures, and it all started with a photo I posted to Instagram.

If you told me a year ago where I would be today, I would have probably thought you were certifiably insane. I had never imagined myself an entrepreneur, owning my own business, working for myself. I had always been on the same track as most— go to college, get a degree, find an internship and, if I am lucky, land a job in my desired field; settling into a cookie-cutter 9 to 5 job, and striving to save enough money to go on one vacation every couple years. Working for someone else's dream, someone else's success, someone else's empire.

But that is surely not how it turned out. In late fall of 2015, I shared a photo on Instagram, wearing a tank from my favourite fitness apparel line, Live Fit Apparel. I was one week away from my second NPC Bikini Competition at the time and was pretty lean... I was showing off my abs in the photo. I had gotten a substantial amount of followers throughout the year from posting fitness-related photos and videos— inspirational quotes, workouts, gym photos, healthy recipes, flexing pictures, etc. People were starting to notice my passion for my sport and for health and fitness, and they followed me for it. They liked seeing my progress and my motivational posts each day. When I posted the photo wearing the Live Fit tank, I "tagged" Live Fit Apparel in the photo. About fifteen minutes later, they "reposted" my photo on their page, wished me good luck at my competition and not long after that I was invited to visit their headquarters for a "trial" photoshoot.

Next thing you know I was their newest signed athlete, making a monthly salary plus commission on sales. This alone was more money than I had ever made before. My social media continued to grow each day, and the exposure I was getting from Live Fit magnified my growth. I started a health and fitness-related YouTube channel, which also began to take off and grow, as my Instagram followers just carried over to YouTube.

That is when I really saw potential in being an entrepreneur and selling myself as a brand— I started a limited liability company, Katie Corio LLC. I threw together my own website (very poorly made due to my lack of experience and technology skills, but I was very proud of my janky site!) and started selling training and nutrition programs online.

As I continued to work on this platform I was moulding for myself, more people started to notice. The thing is, when you truly are passionate about something, it doesn't feel like work! And people notice this passion, and I think that is what attracts people to want to follow you. YouTube especially has helped create a feeling of "friendship" with my subscribers. Watching a video on YouTube is so personal— my subscribers feel like they actually know me, like they are actually my good friends! Just from watching my vlogs about my daily life: school, fitness, competition, my favourite recipes, grocery hauls, talking videos, q&a's, etc. I feel like I can connect with people and help them so much more through a YouTube video than through a photo posted on Instagram.

Anyway... back to the story— my social media continued to boom, and I was soon signed as an athlete with a supplement company, 1Up Nutrition, earning an additional salary plus commission on sales. At this point, I knew the path I was on had potential to be a long-term career for me, and it was my mission to make it so.

Surrendering my homemade website to a professional website developing company, HeartCMS, was the best thing I could have invested in for my business. After working with them for just a month, my sales tripled, my Instagram following increased by more than 30%, and I have a much more credible and legitimate advertisements and SEO strategies. They took the pressure off me trying to make things work smoothly, so I can focus my energy on creating more content and developing new ideas for my business.

This all started with a simple gym-selfie posted up on Instagram! Isn't that just crazy to think about? One year ago I was saving loose change in a ziplock bag under my bed, struggling to have enough money to fill my gas tank each month. Now I am living independently, successfully running my own online business and expecting to make over six figures this year... all before I finish college!

The way that social media has impacted my life is limitless. It is what started my business, how I run my business and how I plan to grow my business and make a comfortable life for myself that I am proud of. It has broken the mould that so much of us fall into— the 9 to 5 boring jobs and living for the weekend. It has not only allowed me to share my passion for health and fitness but it has also allowed me to help others with becoming their best selves... and on top of that, I am making a decent living off of it!

I couldn't be happier and more grateful for the opportunities that social media has presented to me, and how it has positively changed my life.

Katie Corio - www.KatieCorio.com

Becoming A Successful Blogger

Becoming a successful blogger isn't hard, but it isn't going to happen over night. You'll need to have a Google friendly website, set yourself up on social media platforms, write articles for your blog and attend events.

We've packed this book with case studies, information, tips, and hints from our personal experiences of running a UK based marketing company, while blogging ourselves and managing well-known bloggers from around the world. For those of you who are looking at blogging as a form of self-employment and a full-time job, you're in for a treat.

Although we only manage a small percent of the influencers we've managed to help individuals go from 1,000 followers to 10,000 followers and others with 200k followers to one million followers in the space of a few months. Most of our bloggers are making a monthly revenue from blogging varying from £1,000 - £15,000 / month. Not forgetting the bonus of being able to review and keep some awesome products.

Sound awesome? Well once you've made it, it's a nice story to share but until then you've got a lot to do.

Blogging Made Easy

We're going to share with you a journey of a blogger we manage and how she made blogging a full-time job. We need to emphasise that everybody's blogging experience is different. Some don't earn an income until years later. Some start making money within the first six months. Everybody's blogging journey is different.

Also, if you think that you can just start a free-themed blog such as Blogger or WordPress and make money overnight, don't count on it. Monetizing a blog is a step you should take only after several months of solid blogging and when you have at least 5,000 visits a month. Before you step out into the scary world of running ads on your blog and reaching out to brands for collaborations, you should focus on the following;

- Having a Google friendly blog site (which isn't using the same theme as a hundred other bloggers)
- Building great content
- Having an eye-catching design
- Increasing your website traffic.

Once you feel solid with these elements, then you can take a step into building your blog for revenue.

A successful blog accompanies the following two traits of a blogger: One who is skilled and enjoys writing trending articles and one who is great and understands marketing. A blog with great content and a successful marketing strategy can't survive without the other. No one is going to read your blog if your content isn't strong; likewise, no one is going to read your blog if they never come across it.

We've broken down this book into 4 main sections to help you understand the following;

- Importance of a Google friendly blog.
- Social media and how to take advantage of each platform.
- How to reach out and collaborate with brands.
- How to make a living from blogging.

The Importance of A Google & SEO Friendly Blog

To be a successful blogger you need to have a blog site (website), there are no two ways about it. One of the most important elements to having a successful blog online is to have a Google friendly website.

If you already have a blog site which you've designed yourself or had someone build it for you, there's a good chance that parts of it need updating. Using a free theme on a blogging platform such a Blogger or Wordpress will not gain you the results you want. You'll find yourself with minimal organic traffic and rarely any comments.

We receive many enquiries from bloggers asking us to help them with their online marketing, the first action we take is to open and analyse their website. We can confidently say that at least 80% of these blog sites are poorly designed and built on free platforms such as WordPress or Blogger and are not Google friendly.

The most common issues we find are as follows;

- Blog site is not mobile friendly (doesn't resize for different devices)
- No quick contact form / work with me form above the fold
- Top 3 blog posts not mentioned 'above the fold'
- No social media integration
- No Google + account linked
- Slow load speeds
- No blog filters
- No about me page
- Brands i've worked with missing

… and the list goes on.

If you already have a blog site, and you purchased this book because you're having no or limited success, there's a very good chance it's because your blog isn't Google friendly.

Why SEO Matters

SEO (search engine optimisation) is important for your blog for many reasons. We would say the most important reason is to gain traffic and grow your followers. Traffic from search engines can boost the amount of visitors and presence online. This can result in brand collaborations, sponsored reviews and more money from monetising your blog.

SEO brings more people to your blog, rather than just gaining existing followers to visit your website from your social media platforms. SEO helps increase traffic from search engines and these users will be people who don't already follow you, bringing you new social followers the same time. For example if a user searching on Google for a specific search term such as "GHD Straightener review", they are more likely to spend more time on your site as they've hopefully found exactly what they are looking for. Users won't always be on social media to buy products, but they may well be if they are using search engines, which is what brands are looking for.

Have you thought about how you can drive more traffic to your blog? In particular your sponsored posts without having to pay for a boosted post? Then this section of our book is critical.

Most bloggers that we speak to want to gain more brand awareness and organic traffic from search engines but aren't doing the most important things to get traffic using the SEO techniques we are going to talk about and explain in plain English.

Being in the industry and running a fashion and beauty blog on www. hashtagblogger.com, we get a lot of emails from fellow bloggers asking for advice about SEO and optimising their blog for SEO.

Blog Design Tips

Brands looking to work with bloggers have lots of different preferences for how they like blogs to look, and you're never going to please everyone. One thing most brands seem to agree on, however, is that they like the layout to be clean, uncluttered, and easy to navigate.

The fact is, though, that while it's nice to have a great-looking blog, users come for the content, not for the crazy fancy font you want to use in the header or the images in your sidebar. There's nothing wrong with a site with "character" but it's better to try and do that without adding too much clutter. Having a clean website is also good for SEO.

Keep your blog clean, professionally designed and don't use a template. Free and paid templates are not Google approved and if brands come looking and see you have the same blog site as someone else they're likely to leave without getting in touch with you for a collaboration.

This is possibly one of those "goes-without-saying" things, but keeping your design consistent across all of the pages of your blog. This will give it a more cohesive, professional feel. Choose the colours you want to use for your text, logo, headings, etc, and then use them consistently. You'll rarely find a successful blog – particularly a fashion or beauty blog – which uses tiny images, so don't be afraid to make your images big enough to be seen.

This might be somewhat controversial, but we feel strongly enough about it to include it in our book. Use capital letters at the start of sentences and for proper nouns.

The thing is, though, capital letters aren't there to make your sentences look ugly: they help to break up the text, so that when your eye scans it, it's easier to read. A wall of text, all in lower-case, is much harder to read, and no matter how trendy you think it looks, it's making it harder for your readers (and brands) to understand you.

Keep It Compatible

This element of design/development is perhaps one of the most important, and it's about making sure your blog is compatible with different browsers and mobile devices.

A lot of bloggers make the mistake of testing their design only on the browser/ monitor or device they use personally, forgetting that different people (bloggers and brands) use different browsers, differently sized monitors, different resolutions, etc. An increasing number of visitors will also be viewing your blog on their phone or tablet (We do almost all of our blog outreach on mobile devices), so it's really important to make sure your user can actually see and enjoy the content of your blog.

Make sure your blog site is mobile friendly and responsive - come on, it's 2016. If your website isn't mobile friendly, then you might as well not have a website. Online beauty and fashion brands such as TopShop, make most of their sales on mobile devices.

When brands search for bloggers to represent their brands, one of their criteria will be to make sure the blogger has a mobile friendly website. Over 1.2 billion people are accessing the web from mobile devices. That's an incredible 80% of all internet users using a smartphone. In other words, if they're online, they are most likely on their phones.

Google favours mobile friendly and responsive sites and with their latest algorithm updates they have started to penalise sites that aren't mobile-friendly. You'll find most social media referrals, links, images and content are also designed for mobile - so supporting these social links are a no brainer.

A lot of bloggers think having a mobile friendly website is the same as responsive site. That's actually incorrect, a responsive site is where a website re-sizes for a screen such as an iPhone or an iPad.

Going mobile will likely cost time and money and if your blog was created two or more years ago, a new developer might recommend starting from scratch (so you'll be paying for a complete makeover). This is because there are new web development techniques that may make it more efficient to re-do rather than modify your old blog site.

Having a mobile friendly blog consists of the way your website looks and works on a mobile and a tablet device, such as the ones listed below;

Keep menus short and sweet, mobile users and brands visiting your website don't have the patience to scroll through a long list of options to find what they want. Create a mobile friendly menu listing your main navigation links such as Home, About Me, Blog, Work With Me, Contact Me.

Make it easy for the user to navigate back to the home page. Users and brands expect to go back to the homepage when they tap the logo and they become frustrated when it isn't available, or doesn't work.

Make sure your website is developed so it loads as fast as possible, if it takes longer than 3 seconds it's pointless.

You can also check to see if your current website is considered mobile friendly by Google by visiting www.heartcms.com/freetools.

Above The Fold

Above the fold is anything that a user sees once they've landed on your blog. These are the images, texts, forms and content that is immediately visible without scrolling down. Obviously, there are different folds for different laptop and desktop screens. You don't have to worry about that as much, but focus on the things you want people to immediately see once they land on your page, such as your latest blog posts.

Above the fold is uniquely important because it is a new visitor's first impression, but blog familiarity for your returning customers.

What we recommend to advertise above the fold;

- Always advertise your social media icons above the fold. Advertising this helps visitors know you're an established blogger.

- Sliders, build yourself sliders with your own images and add text above them to build eye-catching clickable sliders. These sliders should last no more than 5 seconds per slider and should be clickable to relevant pages/posts.
- Advertise your top 3 posts.
- And of course, all the basic components like your Logo and Navigation.

This doesn't mean that the things below the fold are less important. Below the fold, that's where you put the detailed content. When your visitors are sold on your above the fold impression, they are sure to scroll down and explore the rest of your content and blog posts.

Killer Content

Having great blog content is key and always will be. Content is read not only by your visitors, but also by Brands looking to work with bloggers and Google and other search engines. It's important to write content that is user friendly, appealing and good for SEO.

For many bloggers the about me page is the elephant in the room, and often the most awkward thing to write. It's a shame because over the past few years we have seen that analytics often shows the 'about me' page as one of the most visited pages.

The good news is that the 'about me' page doesn't require lots and lots of paragraphs. Many find it difficult to strike the right balance between selling themselves to their visitors and driving them away with a self-focused approach, which helps explain why the pages are so often neglected. So we thought it would be great to share a few tips when writing content for your about us page.

Start by talking about your audience, not yourself. Dedicate your opening sentence(s) to your audience's challenges and objectives. Starting with the very reason they come to your website in the first place is a good way to demonstrate that you have their needs in mind and your business is there to help solve a problem.

Present your readers with the facts and figures. This could be anything from the brands you have worked with to the number of Instagram followers you have.

Also don't be afraid of where you have come from and your history. If, a year ago, it was your blogging anniversary, celebrate it. The more that people can identify with you, the more trust they'll place in your brand.

SEO Friendly Plugins

When you're first starting off your blog, one of the most exciting yet intimidating things is learning about plugins – what they do, which work, which don't, and which ones you absolutely need.

Plugins are powerful as they are the heart of what makes most blog sites awesome.

WordFence
Someone, one day will try and break into your blog. Wordfence allows you to set parameters about how many times users can attempt to log in before they get locked out. It sends you a notification email when someone attempts to log in using an incorrect login ID or exceeds the number of attempts.

Yoast
One of the most popular SEO plugins out there. Yoast makes it easy to optimise your posts for search engines and installs a form at the bottom of your post page. This form allows you to easily SEO your blog post to gain organic exposure.

More about Yoast and how this plugin works is explained in our 'How To Blog' section.

W3 Total Cache
A slow blog site isn't just super annoying for your readers. It's also bad for SEO. Google's algorithm takes pagespeed into consideration when ranking websites.

W3 Total Cache is a caching plugin. It speeds up your blog site by "increasing server performance, reducing the download times and providing transparent content delivery network (CDN) integration."

We highly recommend you install W3 Total Cache or another caching plugin to speed up your blog site.

Broken Link Checker

The older your blog gets, the more maintenance and cleaning it requires. After a couple of months, you might have old blog posts with links to websites that no longer exist. Or you might have links to a page on your own blog that you've changed the URL for.

One or two broken links may not seem like a big deal, but too many can ruin a reader's experience and hurt your Google rankings.

The Broken Link Checker plugin regularly scans your blog for broken links and notifies you by email when it finds new ones. It compiles all broken links on a single page, making it easy to fix everything in one place.

Setup A Sitemap

Lots of blog sites we look at do not have a site map. You may have heard of Google's Search Console - Webmaster Tools. While your content can still be indexed with Google, using a site map allows you to point where it can be found by search engines such as Google, Yahoo and Bing. This increase the chance and speed of your blog posts being indexed.

Google Analytics

Once your website is up and running you'll want to update it as often as possible. Below we describe two tools you will need to help you analyse and track your website performance.

Google Analytics is one of the most useful free tools you can use when it comes to your blog site.

Google Analytics is basically a free, web-based, tracking and reporting service that allows you to see vital information on how well your blog is performing, which posts get lots of views and which ones get minimal views.

You can see things like; where readers come from (their location), how long they stay for, how they found you and what pages or blog posts are being viewed the most. All super valuable stats that can help you to refine your blog posts and increase engagement.

Installing Google Analytics

Create an account at www.google.com/analytics and click on 'sign into Google Analytics in the top right hand corner to be guided through the set up process.

You'll then need to set up a 'property' which is essentially your website for Google to track.

Set up web tracking and add the Google Analytics tracking ID code (the UA-XXXXXXXX-X number) to your website so that it can start collecting data to show you. To find your tracking ID code in Google Analytics click on the 'Admin' tab then select 'tracking info then 'tracking code' from the middle column headed up as 'Property':

If you need any help with installing Google Analytics to your website please email us at info@heartcms.com.

Using Analytics

Once you've set up Google analytics we recommend giving it a few weeks or so to collect some data but once you've got some data collected in there here are three overview reports to get your started.

Audience Overview

This is the first set of information you'll see once you're logged in. On a basic level it shows you how many visitors have been on your blog in a specific time period. By default Google Analytics shows you the last month of statistics, however, you can change the date range. Simply click on the down-arrow by the date and select the date range you'll like to see.

Here's a quick guide to some of the elements and what they mean;

Sessions - Tell you how many times someone has been on your blog. Every time someone lands on your site, that's counted as a session – whether they viewed one page or multiple pages, this is still counted as one session.

Example: Amy first found your blog on Pinterest and looked at your amazing makeup tutorials. She then came back a couple of days later to re-read one of your posts. Amy has had two sessions on your site.

Users - This is the actual number of people that read your blog in a period of time (by default the last 30 days – but remember you can change the date range!). Whether they're new users or repeat users. So even though Amy has been on your blog twice and accounted for multiple pageviews, she's just the one user.

Page Views - This tells you how many times your site (posts + pages) has been viewed. Not to be confused with how many people have looked at your site – page views is literally how many times any of the pages have been viewed.

Pages / Session - the average number of pages someone views when the visit your site.

Avg. Session Duration - the average length of time that each visitor spends on your website.

Bounce Rate - the percentage of visitors who leave your blog after landing on your homepage (so have only viewed one page).

% of New Sessions - the percentage of people who are visiting your site for the first time (in blue on the pie chart on the right hand side) and the percentage of new visitors are in green.

Acquisition Overview
If you click on 'Acquisition' from the left-hand side navigation menu then select 'overview' this basic report will show you where your blog visitors are coming from.

Social - Ever wonder which social media platforms bring you the most traffic? Analytics does just that and here's where you'll find that answer. Now you can work out which social media platform is actually sending traffic to your website. Use this data to learn which social platforms you should be spending more time on.

Direct - the number of people who just type in your website address to the navigate bar visit your website.

Referral - the number of people being referred to your website from a link on another website.

Organic Search - the number of people who have found your website through a search engine like Google when searching for keywords related to your blog.

Behaviour Overview

Click on 'Behaviour' then 'Behaviour overview' on the left-hand side of your analytics screen to bring up a summary of what content on your site has been most popular in your given date range:

Behaviour overview is a great way to see which of your blog posts are receiving most engagement.

Webmaster Tools

WMT is another free service offered by Google that helps you monitor and maintain your site's presence in Google Search results. A site that's active in Webmaster Tools has a better shot at being fully indexed by Google. There are also a number of deeper insights from Google Webmaster Tools that can be turned into SEO tactical gold. Once you've signed up for an account, login to the Google Webmaster Tools dashboard. From there, you're able to add your site(s). You'll have to first verify that you own the domain. Google provides verification through an easy pop-up process that allows you to login and verify in just a couple of steps.

How To Blog

Let's just get this out of the way, starting your own blog and making it a success is no small task.

There's so much advice out there about what you "should" and "shouldn't be" doing, and it can be damn near impossible to make heads or tails of any of it, especially when you're first starting out. So we've put together a guide based on our experience and Google data to help you kick start your blogging career.

Google, Yahoo and Bing are always improving their algorithms which is why it's important for you as a Blogger to keep up with these SEO demands and blog using Google approved techniques.

Content And Catchy Titles

We know you care about this not only because it affects your blog's SEO, but also because you take pride in writing your blogs. Write your blog content in a natural, helpful tone. Double check your work. A few errors are okay here and there, but remember bad grammar can easily affect how much people enjoy reading your work.

Use attention-grabbing blog post titles. Having a catchy title is the key to grabbing reader's attention. It's your golden ticket to increased traffic and wider audience. You need to elicit interest, emotion, and curiosity in your potential readers to make your blog post title as irresistible as possible. This also plays a crucial role in improving your search ranking of your blog post and other related pages. It's a good idea to search the title you have in mind on Google first. With the sheer number of blogs that exist today, there's a chance that someone has likely used that exact same title. Once you're happy with your post title, you then need to ensure that you use this as a point of reference when developing your content, it will keep you on track and ensure that your content is SEO friendly.

Who is your target audience? What do you think is going to get them interested. If you haven't already, make sure you keep in mind your readers as you begin to develop your blog post. We've often found that when you're writing your headline, the use of numbers can really entice readers in. For example, "My Top 5 Make-Up Tips". Instantly your readers know what they are going to get and possibly get a sense of how long the post is going to be. It's also worth noting that Google will cut off a title that's more than 70 characters long. So keep it short and on point.

Have a think about what you can offer your blog visitors. What's going to make them read that blog title and instantly what to read the full article? Is the blog going to be funny? Informative? Using this technique along with the use of catchy words is really going to help drive traffic to your blog.

Express Your Content

Bloggers love to see the use of illustrations, photographs, drawings, videos and even audio files. They love pretty things. Search engines know that their users (your blog readers) will be happier with posts that include multiple forms of media, instead of just text, so search engines show more love to those posts.

So if you're making a point that is best explained through a video, make a video. Provide a main blog post image that lets people know what your post is about. However, don't forget that you can include more images in the body of the post when they relate to your points.

Our point being if you use different types of content (videos, images, text etc) Google will rank your blog posts higher.

Content That Engages Readers

Search engines want to show your readers websites that are interesting and that the readers will spend a lot of time on. Google and other search engines pay attention to how engaging a blog's content is, they are improving their algorithms to identify interactive, captivating sites more and more.

Engage your blog readers through great content, images, a logical layout, an easy-to-use site, and your personality and jokes. Your blog's search engine rankings will thank you. If you're able to keep people on your site longer than other sites, search engines such as Google will love you.

Divide Up Your Content Into Smaller Sections

When we see a blog with enormous blocks of text — even if it's something we're interested in — we usually just find something that's more formatted for reader sanity. Try to include no more than 5-6 lines of text in your paragraphs and divide up sections with larger headlines.

Many readers will scan through a post, see if it sounds useful to them, and then decide if they'll actually read the whole thing. By using big blocks of text with no headlines, you're making it hard for readers to see what your post is actually about.

SEO Friendly Content

Making sure your blog content is SEO friendly is extremely important. This will affect your blog's placement on search engines. If you're landing on the first page you increase the likelihood of gaining shares, likes and comments.

Use headlines and Sub-headings. Along with your catchy headline that we've covered previously, sub headings make your content easier to read as your visitors will be able to skim the text. Users are far more likely to share a blog post that is easy to read. Plus, the big bonus is that sub headings can increase the number of times you are using your main keywords throughout.

Add links to previous posts. Linking back to previous articles is a great way to increase the time users spend on your site. The time on site has a direct impact on rankings, so make sure, where applicable this is done. There's also an advantage to linking your article to reputable and highly regarded sources. This will build trust with your visitors.

Make it readable. Google will give precedent to longer articles, however, you must tread carefully, as the longer the article is, you increase your chances of losing readers. Aim for a minimum of 350 words and try not to go too far over 1,000. Keep in mind your keywords, in a post this length, try and hit between 5-10 keywords. Make sure you choose your keywords wisely.

SEO Friendly URLS

The URL of your blog post is an important ranking factor. You need it to be descriptive but as brief as possible. You want your visitors to have a good idea of what they are going to read just from looking at the URL. Keep your URL focussed, it's a good idea to get rid of words like 'a', 'the', 'of' and so on. You can even remove verbs such as 'are' and 'have'. None of these words will add value to your URL.

Example of a good URL:

http://www.hashtagblogger.com/summer-essentials-tips/

Examples of bad URLs:

http://www.hashtagblogger.com/tips/

http://www.hashtagblogger.com/?11343-dfdwe/

Giveaways And Competitions

Running a competition is a great way of promoting your blog and encouraging traffic to your website or social media. There's a number of ways you can collect entries including 'like and share', blog comments, newsletter sign ups and 'caption this'. The aim is to either drive new readers to your site, or increase the number of likes or follows. The main thing here, is to ensure the prize you're giving away is enticing enough to get them to do what you'd like them to do. However, you don't want people entering who just love a competition, you want to encourage new followers who are going to love your content, so make sure it's relevant to what you do.

Add "alt text" To Your Images

You include images in your articles to get people to read your text. Well-chosen images also strengthen your message. You shouldn't forget to give those images good alt attributes: alt tags and title tags strengthen the message towards search engine spiders and improve the accessibility of your website.

The alt and title attributes of an image are commonly referred to as alt tag or alt text and title tag even though they're not technically tags. The alt text describes what's on the image and the function of the image on the page. So if you have an image that's used as a button to buy product X, the alt text would say: "button to buy product X".

The alt tag is used by screen readers, the browsers used by blind and visually impaired people, to tell them what is on the image. The title attribute is shown as a tooltip when you hover over the element, so in case of an image button, the button could contain an extra call-to-action, like "Buy product X now for $19!".

Each image in your article should have an alt text. Not just for SEO purposes but also because blind and visually impaired people otherwise won't know what the image is for. A title attribute is not required. It can be useful but in most cases, leaving it out shouldn't be much of an issue.

Social Sharing

Social sharing links are a great way to get your posts out there. If you don't already have them on your blog then download a plugin called Social Warfare. The more people that share your posts, means the more readers it will reach, all resulting in an increase in engagement on your posts.

Does your content get shared by your readers or visitors? Is your content worth reading? All of the best tips in the world won't help you if it's not. So spend some time on nailing this and then follow some of our tips to help optimise your website for social media sharing.

Display your social shares. Are your social shares clearing displayed on your articles? Can visitors share your posts on their social media channels at the click of a button? If not, then make sure you action this ASAP, this will only increase your chances of it being shared.

Create good metadata. Make sure you add good Metadata to your blogs. This will ensure when a user shares your posts on their social media channels it will be visually appealing, with an appropriate image and description.

Optimise your social images . There's no one size fits all job for sharing posts on social media. Twitter, Facebook, Instagram, Pinterest etc. So spend some time optimising your images.

Be consistent. Regardless of how many followers you have, make sure you post regularly. This will get you noticed. People are more likely to follow and engage with you if they see that you are active on your blog and posting them on your social media channels.

Promote your blog. Once you've posted your latest blog. What are you doing to promote it? We've put together a list of ways we find have the biggest impact when it comes to sharing your blog.

Promote via social media. Every time you create a new blog post, you need to ensure that you're sharing it on each of your social channels. Don't be afraid of sharing your post more than once, providing it's not seasonal, remind your followers a week or even a few months later. Don't worry about spamming your followers. Social media is so fast paced these days, it's likely they'll only see it once.

Build an email list. If you haven't already got a newsletter sign up or subscription platform, make it a priority. Now, you don't want to spam your email list every single time you post a new blog, this will likely lead to un-subscribers. But you could consolidate your blogs into one short newsletter and send it once a month.

Pin Your Post On Pinterest

Since you've already added your "alt text" for your images before inserting them into your post, the description is already written. Now, all you have to do is pin your blog post image onto Pinterest.

We recommend creating a Pinterest board specifically for your blog (We have one called "Hashtag Blogger"), which only shares pins from your own posts. Pin your blog post images onto that board first. Then, over the next couple days, pin them onto other relevant boards with a medley of pins from your blog and from other sources. This will keep your pin in rotation and distribute it to different audiences (who may be following different boards).

Live Stream Your Blog Post

Periscope and Snapchat is quickly becoming a "thing" that bloggers do. It's a pretty awesome and fun way to connect with all of the other bloggers who share the same interest.

The great thing about Periscope and Snapchat is that it gives you a different medium to share your content. Some people enjoy reading blog posts. Others would prefer to watch them. So, after you publish your post, try doing a Periscope video about your post's topic. You already wrote the post, so your "script" is finished! Obviously, I don't recommend just reading your post word for word, but share the main points of it on Periscope and/or Snapchat and get people hyped to read the full post on your blog. This is an excellent way to repurpose older content, too.

Respond To Comments

If your post receives any comments, make an effort to respond to them, especially if people have questions or are extra thoughtful.

Responding to comments is a great way to build a stronger readership, more engagement, and friendships with readers who will come back because you make them feel valued.

Guest Blogging

Another great way of using someone else's audience. This can be achieved by publishing a post right on their blog. It's a great way to get your name out there and drive some traffic to your site. Make sure you're targeting the correct audience and don't forget to leave a link back to your blog and social media.

Have you signed up to be be featured on Hashtag Blogger? Head over to our website to find out more. http://www.hashtagblogger.com/write-for-us/

You should also spend some time building a relationship with other bloggers and use it as an opportunity to appear in front of their audience. Make sure you leave something helpful, funny or insightful. You want to ensure you grab the attention of the author and their readers. Why not leave a link back to your blog in the comment too.

Monetise Your Blog

Most bloggers write primarily as a hobby or because they enjoy it; whether or not they make money from their blog doesn't make too much of a difference. Other bloggers, however, write seriously in hopes of making an income and becoming the next Zoella.

For these bloggers, being able to count on a certain amount of money each month through their blogs is important.

Here are a few ways you can make a steady income by blogging. Bear in mind that how much profit you make from your site each month will depend largely on how much time you invest in your blog, how many different ways you monetize your site, and how large of an audience your site reaches.

Guest Blogging

So we've touched base on guest blogging already but now we explain how guest blogging can help make you make money. Guest posting for other sites might not jump out as an effective way of monetizing your blog, but in the long run, you can develop a steady stream of income by guest posting. Many blogs pay for guest posts. If you agree to regularly guest post each month for a blog that pays you to be a contributor, you could make anywhere from £50-£100 for the articles you write, depending on the blog. It might not be much, but it's something you can rely on.

Additionally, guest posting is a great way of getting your name as a writer out there and driving traffic back to your blog, which increases the income you make through affiliate advertising and pay-per-click advertising. Most articles you write will include a link back to your blog, along with a short bio about you as a writer. This encourages readers who enjoy your posts to go visit your blog. You can also usually include links within your guest posts to posts on your own blog – just double check with the blog owner to make sure this is allowed before doing so. Avoid turning a guest post into a series of links; make sure the post has enough information to stand alone, but include a few links that give interested readers more in-depth information or resources related to the topic of the article.

Sponsored Posts

Working with brands to write sponsored posts is another way to make money as a blogger. Sponsored posts and reviews can be fun and gives you the opportunity to build long-term relationships with brands so you can collaborate with them over and over again.

You can work with brands directly by emailing them or you can join networks that will connect you with brands that fit with your blog and target audience. If you haven't already, you should sign up to our very own blogger's network - www.hashtagblogger.com.

Figure out how much you will charge and what types of brands you would like to work with. You do not want to work with a brand that has nothing to do with your blog just because they will pay you.

At times it can be difficult to know what to charge for a sponsored review, this is because the rates change daily. For this reason, we can't provide a guide price because by the time this book goes to our publishing team, gets published and printed the rates will have changed. However, we can indicate that the bloggers we manage charge anywhere from £100 - £4,000 per sponsored article.

You need to know when to say yes and when to say no because you are building your brand with your blog. Keep in mind that a lot of brands will have specific requirements that you will need to adhere to.

You want to make sure that you are comfortable with their terms before accepting a sponsored post. You may find that you do not have a lot of creative freedom for the article, and some brands can get a little upset if you re-word their pitching statements.

Don't forget, nearly all brands require a certain amount of monthly page views or social media followers before offering sponsored content. So make sure you've done everything else mention in this book before you go out reaching for collaborations.

Sell A Service or Product

Selling a product through your website is probably one of the best and smartest methods to making money while blogging.

We know, it seems like weird advice coming from us as we don't actually 'sell' anything on our website, but trust us – it's something we've done and worked on with the bloggers we manage and products are flying out.

So… what should you sell? If you're crafty, you could create things and sell them on Etsy/eBay and of course link them on your blog. If you're a skilled designer, you can consider offering those services to other bloggers – selling blog designs, banners or logos. If you're a good writer, try getting freelance gigs through your website.

Some bloggers also teach blogging courses, but for this, you need to be very advanced and experienced. And that's not all – being an expert at something doesn't mean you'll also be good at teaching that thing. Teaching is a skill, and it's not as common as people tend to believe.

Try to pinpoint what you're excellent at – the things that make you stand out – and figure out how you could sell that as a product or service. There is no one-size-fits-all answer here, and you need to analyse your skills and find ways to monetise them.

The key is using your blog to reach potential clients and then market your services to them. Subtly. Do not convert your blog into a horrible marketing page. If your blog loses its soul, we can guarantee your readers will notice and that they will not be happy.

Sponsored Giveaways

Sponsored giveaways aren't too different from sponsored posts, but we decided to make them into a separate section to remind you that (if you have a large engaged audience) they are something you can be charging for as well.

How much you charge can depend on many factors including the value of the giveaway, what the company are asking for and what you and your followers get out of it in return.

Do what feels right – you don't always need to ask for money and if you do, you always need to justify why you should be paid for the post.

Google Adsense

Turn your passion into profit with Google Adsense. AdSense is a free, simple way to earn money by placing ads on your website.

Most bloggers assume you need high traffic to make anything from Google AdSense. The answer is simple, yes if you have 100,000s of pageviews a month you will earn a decent amount from AdSense, but that's not to say that if you receive a lot less that you can't earn through Adsense as that most definitely isn't true!

When we first installed AdSense to our website when we first started blogging. Our traffic was less than 10,000 page views a month and we still made £1 a day here and there and other days we made a few pennies which we were quite pleased with as our blog was basically making money as we slept. Fast forward three months and we now earn a decent amount from Google AdSense.

How to sign up for Google AdSense

1. Go to http://google.com/adsense and click the start button.

2. You must have a Google account, a website or blog in which to place ads, and a mailing address.

3. Walk through the setup process and await confirmation from Google of your acceptance or rejection. This can take a few days.

Did you know that where and how you place your ads makes a whole lot of difference between earning pennies and pounds a day? Ensure you have at least one ad showing above the fold.

You might be tempted to use a plugin for Google AdSense once you receive your acceptance. While some of the plugins have nice functionality, we always suggest doing things without one if you can.

There are three places you want to consider putting your ads – on the sidebar, right at the top of your pages (under or above the header), and somewhere in the content (either at the end near the footer, before the comments, or right in the middle of the text).

It's important not to forget about mobile phone users. In some cases, ads on mobile are very annoying for your readers because they don't line up correctly, or they make it impossible to scroll through content without having to close out boxes. The best places to put your ads on your mobile site are either directly in the header or footer and in and around your articles. For example, take a look at www.rumenabegum.com.

Once you've signed up to Google AdSense and installed it to your blog site, be sure to checkout our weekly AdSense tips over at www.hashtagblogger. com.

Social Media

Social media has changed the world of SEO and online marketing. In the last couple of years, many social media marketing companies are coming into the market to create brand awareness via Social media promotion.

There was a time when traffic to a website was only dependent on a search engine. Now, the scenario has completely changed and internet marketers and Bloggers are using social media marketing strategies to tap targeted traffic from social media sites such as Facebook, Twitter and Google+.

Being a Blogger you have already achieved the first milestone in your social media presence and now it's time to move to leverage the power of these social media platforms and turn it into your profit. From a Blogger perspective, it will be idle if you are driving traffic and converting them into subscribers/ followers. From a brand perspective, getting feedback from user/customer and engaging them in your social media campaign should be the first objective.

Not every social media platform is a great investment of your time as a blogger. Especially when you consider where your audience is, how they use each platform, your own brand culture, and the available time you have to maintain each account.

As a blogger, marketing on social media sites will directly help in more traffic, more links, better PR, Better Alexa rank and other traffic rank and most important more subscribers.

Social Media Do's

- Engage with users
- Post in a scheduled manner
- Post daily or regular interval
- Share links/images/video related to your niche
- Keep an eye on social media trends and upcoming sites in your niche
- Talk about trending topics

- Keep your profile information up to date
- Target users based on demographic and interest
- Monitor brand presence on social media sites
- Add humour and add a personal touch into your updates and comments
- Keep an eye on competitor strategies
- Increase trust, loyalty and brand awareness

Which Platforms Are Good For Blogging

As a beauty or fashion blogger you ideally need to be on most of the social media platforms available. We'll explain each individual platform, how they work, the benefits of using them and a few tips and tricks to get you started.

With all popular social media sites being mobile-friendly, this makes it easy for your followers to engage with your Facebook page, scroll through tweets and check out a pin from Pinterest.

All these reasons suggest that engagement across social networks is never going to end; rather, users will keep on Instagramming, Tweeting or Liking – or doing whatever the next big social media platform will decide.

As a new person to blogging, you may think you need a big budget to get your blog up and running. But, your social media marketing strategy doesn't have to be expensive.

What's great about social media is it's easy to set up and once you're on various social media platforms, you'll find you can reach a wide audience without spending much on analytics and boosting.

Social media is here to stay and it's not a passing phase. Let's uncover how to strategise each social media platform with a few tips to get you started.

Instagram

Instagram is a social media photo sharing app with over 500 million users. It enables it's users to take pictures and videos and share them with their followers online. This can be done either publicly or privately.

One of Instagrams most used features are it's filters, allowing users to transform their images. Instagram can be connected to your existing social profiles such as Facebook and Twitter meaning you can share your photos across all your social platforms.

In their latest update, Instagram have introduced the use of stories where users can post a number of photos and videos in on stream. This is very similar to the way Snapchat stories works, where this stream will disappear after 24 hours. Stories are not posted to the user's feed and follow the privacy settings of that account.

Why Use Instagram

What do we think at Hashtag Blogger? Well, Instagram is our favourite social media platform, it's an amazing way for us to reach potential bloggers and communicate with our followers. Unlike Facebook, Instagram does not separate Business pages and Personal pages. It's all together in one feed and we don't believe the chronological manner of Instagram attributes to increased engagement for ourselves. The average Instagram user follows around 822 profiles. Unless you are posting frequently throughout the day (which is a bad idea anyway) the likelihood of them seeing your post is slim.

The great thing is that Instagram have been kind enough to warn us about these upcoming changes. Spend some time increasing engagement on your profile now. The more engagement you create, the more likely you are to end up at the top of one of your followers feeds. Engage with your following, like their photos, respond to comments, ask questions to encourage them to comment on your photos.

If you want to have more comments and likes, have you tried asking for them? Ask your followers what they think of your latest post, this is more likely to strike up a conversation. Ask them what they think and see if it works. Why not run a hashtag contest? Ask your followers to upload a picture or comment with a specific hashtag. Get it trending, and this will all lead more people to your social media profiles.

We talk more about the importance of engagement rates, later on in the book.

Having great content is key and always will be. Content is read not only by your visitors, but also by Google and other search engines. It's important to write content that is user friendly, appealing and good for SEO.

Spend money wisely on Instagram ads to give yourself a boost, but always have a focus on catchy imagery that will engage your followers.

What Does Rumena Think of Instagram

Instagram is such a powerful tool, use it to your advantage. I am where I am today because of my Instagram. Most people are using Instagram as a marketing mechanism for their business. I feel like Instagram is an app most people use every single day whether it's posting pictures/videos, browsing or promoting, it has become a beneficial tool for everyone. Instagram is most definitely the reason why I started blogging. When I first started off I uploaded posts on my page daily and the more you upload, the more engagement you'll receive.

It's very important you interact with your followers and listen to what they say. My followers suggested I start a YouTube channel and that's exactly what I did. Most of my subscribers are from Instagram. The more interaction you have with your followers the better for you as these individuals will grow fond of you and will constantly keep up to date with your posts.

Only upload posts that relate to you. If you're a blogger it's all about you! It's pointless uploading random shoutouts that have absolutely nothing to do with you. Be very selective with the posts you upload. Understand that people follow you for you, so just do you!

How To Setup And Manage Instagram

Create A Killer Instagram Profile
- Recognisable & Searchable @Username for example @Rumena_101

Don't make it difficult for users to find you by having a complicated or really long username. If possible use your business name, or if for example you're a personal trainer. Your name. If your name is taken, try incorporating some industry related works e.g. @GarethJamesPT @GarethJamesFitness

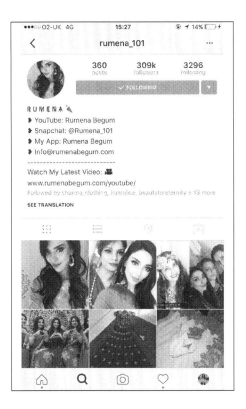

- Searchable profile name

Ensure that you have entered your full business name into your profile.

- Profile image (head shot or logo)

Your profile is the first thing that users will see so you want it to be on point. Either use your logo, or a photo of yourself. You'll notice from the image here, that the profile image is circular, you don't have any say in this, so make sure when setting up your logo that everything you want user to see stays within that circle.

- Informative Bio

Same as your logo, this is the first thing a user will see. Make sure you use up all 150 characters that are available to you to really sell your profile, who are you? what do you do? why are you different?

- Change the link in your bio regularly

The only place on your Instagram page that you can place a link that takes the user away from your profile is the one in your bio. You want to be using your social media as a tool to drive traffic to your blog posts.

Using Instagram As A Microblogging Platform

By using Instagram to microblog and share small updates and valuable content with your followers – you'll see an increase in your engagement (likes, followers and comments).

We've talked before about the importance of sharing original content on Instagram, as opposed to only sharing the same things you post to your blog. In this regard, we think turning more towards the idea of Instagram as a microblogging platform an excellent way to win new followers.

Microblogging allows you to focus on different areas that you might not be able to talk in-depth about on your blog site. For example, we mostly blog about blogging, branding, and creative business nowadays, but we still use our Instagram to share lifestyle updates, DIY projects, decor, recipes, etc. because we still love to share these things. We've begun thinking of Instagram more as my micro-blog than just another social media site.

Essentially, it's a better way to strategize content on Instagram, an area that many bloggers still struggle with. Here are some suggestions for ways to utilise this thought process into your Instagram strategy.

Share bite-sized tidbits of information or tips related to that day's blog post to engage your audience further and to reach new viewers. You can easily create infographics or simply use the caption and comments of a similarly themed photo/image to convey the message.

You want to be sure you're adding lots of value for your followers and readers. You should never do something just for the sake of posting a post, or worse, because you think it will be "trending" enough to get you noticed. These attempts are always transparent, and your followers will not think highly of them.

Depending on your target audience, create a simple recipe tutorial, make-up tutorial, or a shop this look to share on Instagram. It's the perfect visual type of content, and the hashtag system will ensure that it is seen by more viewers than ever. (For a list of effective hashtags, check out our website www.hashtagblogger.com)

If you've shared a recipe or make-up tutorial on your blog, then post a photo to Instagram of you or your family or friends enjoying the end product. If you're a fashion blogger, share photos from behind the scenes of your photoshoots, or share "outtakes" that didn't quite make the cut on your blog.

Push Notifications

You really want to show your potential followers that you're an active and dynamic blogger. You can achieve this partly by always being active on Instagram, engaging with your followers and responding to comments and likes. To ensure you're always on top of this, ensure you've got Push Notifications turned on.

Engage With Your Followers

Here are some simple mistakes to avoid as part of your social media marketing efforts.

1. Don't miss your target audience

Have you targeted the correct demographics? If you have, are you posting high quality content that they want to engage in? There's really no point in having followers that don't engage or aren't interested in the things you post. So don't miss your audience.

2. Don't forget to build a relationship

New likes, follows and comments are great and look good. But building a long term relationship with your followers is key. Are you engaging with them? Responding or liking their comments? If not, you're missing a huge part of building longevity with your followers.

3. Don't always push paid products or ads

Have you thought about running a competition? Have you done products giveaways? This is a great way of getting your brand/product out there and being used. Also, if your followers see your page full of paid posts and advertisements they will soon switch off. It's important you're careful with the types of content you post. Does it fit with what you'd usually talk about? Will your followers lose trust in you as a result. Remember, your followers will follow you for you.

Instagram Tips

First and foremost you need to make sure you fully understand reach. It's essentially the amount of people who can view your posts at any one time. If you have 3000 followers, you have the potential to have a reach of 3000 people. Straightforward right?

If you've seen a dip in your engagement, here's some tips to help you out.

Split Test/Experiment

The main things you want to be considering when you post is the content the caption and the time. Mix up your approach to these three things and figure out which works best.

1. Don't just use one type of content – Mix up the content that you use, post videos, asks questions of your audience, use funny quotes and see which gets the most engagement.
2. Don't post at the same time every day – Try posting at different times during the day and make sure you monitor the times where your engagement is best.
3. Are your captions too long? Are they too short? Mix up the length of your captions and see which works best.
4. Are you seeing results from the hashtags you are using? If not, do some research and see what's trending to really figure out which is best.

Hashtags

You're far better off focusing on killer content and using appropriate and relevant hashtags to really drive engagement. Try split testing some hashtags and see what works best. Unlike Twitter, you do not have a character limit, so use a few hashtags if you need to.

By using these hashtags, the image is saved so other Instagram users who search for images related to #Blogging can find it.

Industry or Brand Specific Hashtags

If you are running a particular campaign try using unique hashtags to drive traffic to the specific posts you would like users to see. Also look into what is currently trending in your industry and make sure you incorporate these into your posts.

Ask For Comments And Likes

If you want to have more comments and likes, have you tried asking for them? Ask your followers what they think of your latest post, this is more likely to strike up a conversation. Ask them what they think and see if it works. Why not run a hashtag contest? Ask your followers to upload a picture or comment with a specific hashtag. Get it trending, and this will all lead more people to your social media profiles.

Promote Your Killer Content

Having great content is key and always will be. Content is read not only by your visitors, but also by Google and other search engines. It's important to write content that is user friendly, appealing and good for SEO.

Spend money wisely on Facebook ads to give yourself a boost, but always have a focus on catchy imagery that will engage your followers.

Engage With Your Followers

When users comment, are you responding? Are you engaging them in order to strike up a conversation? If you're not, get on it now. Most users will have their favourite celebrities or brands that they follow, and they most likely load up Instagram and go straight to their page to see what's new. I know I do.

Time Your Social Posts For Maximum Engagement

Another thing to consider is the time you post. Is it at the optimum moment when you're really going to get the maximum out of your post engagement? Get to know your industry and find out when, how and what should be posted. Are you using analytics to follow the trends of your engagement?

Things To Avoid

1. Incorrect Hashtags

There are hundreds of thousands of hashtags on Instagram. They are everywhere. Some hashtags get abused also. Yes, using the most popular hashtags will extend the reach of your posts and reach a larger audience. But, it's important they are relevant to the content, if they're not then don't use them.

If you're using too many hashtags our your posts (or spamming). This is sure to get you struck off Instagrams high quality list. It's important that you're using the most relevant and specific hashtags. The idea is that you're helping people find exactly what they're looking for. This will pay off eventually.

2. Too Many Hashtags

As we've mentioned above, spamming your posts with loads of hashtags is a bad idea for a number of reasons. You need to ensure you are using the most relevant hashtags. This will ensure your posts looks professional and this will pay off in they eyes of your followers.

We recommend limiting your hashtags to around 5 per post. Better still, use one and comment on your own post with up to 5 more. This leaves your post looking top quality and easy to find.

3. Too Many Posts

Accounts posting content too often is a common mistake and something that is sure to make your follower hit that unfollow button. Avoid posting two images in a row and be strategic in the times you post.

4. Poor Quality Images

Cut off text, blurry images and re posting of low quality quotes are just a few mistakes people make. Spend some time to create high quality content.

5. No Structure

Think about generating some sort of theme to your posts. If you're completely random your followers may not really understand what it is you stand for. We've certainly noticed that accounts that have a theme and look professional tend to get more engagement. Of course, it's ok to go off piste with your theme now and then, but it's important you're consistent.

Instagram Analytics

There are a number of free tools available on the internet to track your Instagram Analytics. One that we would recommend is Iconosquare.

It's a desktop app that provides some pretty in-depth analytics, which included the total number of likes received, your most liked photos and the number of likes and comments you're receiving. It gives you growth follower charts and more.

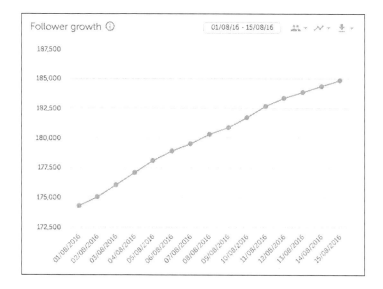

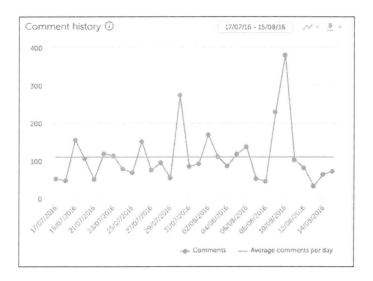

What HB Ambassador Katie Hall Thinks of Instagram

My love for this blogging world started when I discovered Nicole Guerriero on youtube at the age of 14. I was instantly hooked! I loved that she could just sit in front of a camera and talk about makeup and do makeup looks for everyone to see. From that moment on I was addicted.

I have always known I was into makeup however I thought that was just how girls were and that it wouldn't be a career for me. I then started becoming more creative, testing colours and techniques for nights out or special events and always had people commenting on my makeup.

I decided to start my blog 'The Beauty Hall' a few years ago, however, started off just talking about beauty and fashion and I didn't post any of my makeup looks. I feel like becoming a blogger happens in steps/stages, it doesn't just happen overnight. I was always doing makeup for friends and family and decided I had to post one of my looks. I didn't get much more feedback than I would with the regular beauty posts so decided I needed to take the plunge and share my blog on Instagram and Facebook. Once I did this I noticed my views going up a lot higher. It also gave me the spur to keep going. Noticing that people were watching and interested in my makeup looks made me want to post more regular and creative looks. It quickly picked up from there and

I soon became obsessed, posting at least once a week and saving for a new camera to take better pictures so I could create better content for my followers.

Blogging really does have to be something you love and enjoy. I bought myself a new camera for my 20th birthday and decided to step things up a notch, I even tried vlogging my birthday weekend in Manchester. Although never seen by my readers I kept it as I loved that I could look back at such an amazing weekend. I feel like that is a very significant point in my life, that's when I realised I wanted blogging to be my career and I would do anything it takes to make it happen. Although still on that journey and not there yet I feel like I have come such a long way from that weekend back in Feb 2016.

I started actively looking for more and more ways to get myself seen and discovered that there were companies like Hashtag Blogger around that took bloggers under their wings and helped to transform their careers and give them the push they needed. Most ask for a blog post to feature and will either just feature the post on their site the once or they will ask you to become an ambassador. After sending so many posts and emails through I was lucky enough to have my post featured on the Hashtag Blogger website. I was so happy and over the moon with my achievement! I woke up the next morning from another email from Hashtag Blogger. I couldn't believe my eyes when they asked me to become a brand ambassador. That whole day was a blur from the excitement. Being a brand ambassador for HTB means that I get sent free products to review for them and that I write a blog post for them every week. We also get invited to exclusive events with brands which will help us to network even more.

My favourite Social Media platform has to be Instagram. I just love that I can post pictures of all of my looks and what I get up to. It is almost like an online gallery/portfolio of my life. If you want to get noticed as a beauty blogger, MUA or anything for that matter I think it is important that your profile is public. No one will want to follow you if they don't know what you post about. I get so much inspiration from Instagram, you can find so many different people with so many different interests and I love finding new MUA's to follow. 9/10 times when doing a makeup look it is because I have seen something on Instagram that has inspired me to do it. It is such a great way of getting noticed and sharing your passion with people.

If you are thinking of becoming a blogger I would say just do it! If you know you are passionate about it then what is the harm in trying? If people pick on you for it ignore them! If you're good at it and enjoy it then do it. I also think that mind manipulation is a very strong thing. If you truly believe you can do something and want to do something and think about it enough, eventually you will manipulate life to make you succeed and achieve what you want in life. Anyone will be a hard worked when it comes to something they love! Never give up and always keep positive!

Katie Hall - www.instagram.com/katieha11

What HB Ambassador Sophie Charlton Thinks of Instagram

My name is Sophie Charlton, I am 21 years old and I have been blogging for over a year now, I first started blogging during my final year at University. My favourite foundation is NARS sheer glow, I have an unhealthy obsession with River Island and I am a marketing graphic designer. I remember 3 years ago I became obsessed with these beauty and fashion bloggers that I discovered through my Instagram feed, around this time I also became more and more drawn to different YouTubers. This was my first big eye opener when I realised people were doing this for a living and absolutely loving it. I didn't have a clue that people even blogged till then let alone blogging full time. The more I delved into YouTube the more I became obsessed with the world of the beauty industry. I blame bloggers/You Tubers for the amount products I have purchased over the years. I remember the endless amount of hours I was sat glued watching these beauty gurus talking about new product launches and vlogging their daily lives, I really was hooked. I think the more spare time I had at University the more I watched and read content being put out there by these amazing beauty gurus.

For ages, I knew I wanted to start my own blog but it really took me a while to bite the bullet and go for it because I believed that people who knew me in real life wouldn't understand and turn their nose up at it. If there's one thing I've learnt it is to not hold back, do not care about others passing judgement and do what makes you happy. A little cliché I agree but all so true at the same time because if I didn't go for it back then I probably would have pushed it aside and never got round to it due to my lack of confidence. Even though I haven't been blogging for that long I have definitely noticed a difference in my own content, photography and general engagement. There are many things you learn through blogging especially when it comes to making your own a success, but what really counts is that you enjoy creating this content. I am generally a creative person there is nothing more I enjoy than designing, drawing, creating photography and so on; therefore creating beautiful images and writing content about a passion I have for a particular industry is amazing and such a fun process.

When it comes to blogging social media platforms can be your best friend. Not only do you want your audience to engage with you through your blog but also through your social media so you can connect with them more! A lot of people are able to find and read your blog through your social media platforms so it is vital to get signed up to all these platforms such as Twitter, Instagram, Facebook and Blog Lovin.

My favourite platform at the minute is Instagram, I love engaging with other bloggers images it's so pleasing and therapeutic to scroll through in the evenings. This is a great way to display a theme of photographs and really sell yourself and your blog. Immediately I can say the main reason why I am drawn to this platform more than others is because I am such a visual and creative person. There is so much to explore through Instagram, not only is it a platform for people to post whatever they like but it's a place for people to really express their creativity and engage with followers through the love of imagery. I think your Instagram feed can say a lot about your personality and what you are interested in, so following others who post similar imagery or really go that extra mile to post amazing content that coincides with their blog can help you engage a lot with others. I also love how themes can be incorporated into your Instagram feed, what I mean by a theme is by expressing a collective amount of posts/photographs which may have similar backgrounds, saturated editing, or the same filters even which allows them to all work amongst each other under a 'theme'. Mine for example currently has the same editing features applied to each image, with the photographs often having a white background.

One of my tips to increase engagement and followers using Instagram is to avoid uploading out of focus and dark images, of course, everything is personal preference, however, uploading clear crisp and brightly lit images are much more aesthetically pleasing to look at. Taking full attention to detail with your photography can be a huge thing when it comes to engaging with others and making your platform and blog a success. You don't have to be an amazing photographer from the very beginning, most bloggers have started from the bottom and taught themselves to better their images so don't panic. Comparing my old photograph's to now you can see a huge difference in quality and that all comes with practice and time. For example when taking photographs of products you need to think about the background, keep it simple, dress it up a little bit, maybe use different textures. I love to use white backgrounds a lot it really makes the products stand out a lot more and makes it the main focus. If you have good quality photographs people tend to become more engaged with your posts, if you have blurry and out of focus images it can become slightly off-putting. Natural lighting can be key to successful photography even if you are new to it. Having good natural lighting allows your images to remain well lit, especially if you are placing them on white backgrounds! Also, play around with different types of shots from different angles until you are satisfied with a few, close up shots of products are great as your followers will really want to see your main focus of your images clearly.

Another tip is to post regularly and to make sure that the content you are putting out there is relevant to you and your blog. This of course isn't essential as it's up to you what you post on Instagram but if you want to stay active and continue to grow your platform then posting relevant content is very important as your existing followers have followed you for a reason and that is to see more photographs related to your blog and interests. Staying active and posting up to 4 times a day can really help this as it shows you are willing to engage with your audience. Using hashtags that are appropriate and relate to what you're passionate about can help target new users on Instagram to view your uploads, for example popular hashtags related to the beauty industry such as #bbloggers will show all the photographs uploaded on Instagram with the use of this particular hashtag.

If I could give one tip to someone who wanted to be a blogger it would be to really go that extra mile and enjoy everything you do. Make sure that the content you create is content that you would love to read, make sure that your photography is something that you would love to see on someone else's blog. Really focus on your creative side and let your experimental skills loose! If you're not passionate about what you're blogging about then your readers will be able to notice, this could be due to lack of attention to detail in your photographs, how active you are on social media and your blog, your ability to proofread and create interesting fun content. So really push yourself and remember to enjoy it and have fun!

Sophie Charlton - www.instagram.com/sophiecharlton1

What Instakicksz Thinks Of Instagram

Started in September 2015 as a sneaker enthusiast, first established to help other people find rare and exclusive sneaks that are not available in store.

The name was influenced by social media platform 'Instagram'. By using this platform for exposure, we have been able to become a recognised business and brand, gained loyal customers and consumer trust; we also have regular customers who buy from us over and over again, and we never slip on the quality of service despite how busy and quick our growth is becoming. This platform has also given us the opportunity to work with the many household names on Instagram.

We have worked alongside social media influencers such as Sarah Ashcroft, a blogger who promotes brands and shares her opinion to her followers about her experiences of services and products.

Also, One of our first customers now a very good friend, celebrity car customizer. Yiannimize - with Instagram followers near to 1 Million, Yiannimize has a big social media presence to a range of potential customers.

As a promoted and trusted brand, we look for a few characteristics in bloggers, this includes:

- Social media presence
- People with the same / similar target audience
- Who has a lot of engagement with followers
- Who uphold a positive and respectable reputation

Snapchat is also another platform which our bloggers and influencers make use of when receiving goods; the short 24 hour lasting videos enable fans to view the packaging and first-hand view of how the recipient is feeling about the product and service, this not only makes the target audience feel engaged but also makes them feel involved as most bloggers would ask their followers for their opinion. We also ship worldwide, therefore by using Instagram, pictures are easier to share from any location.

As we had only just started in 2015, we are looking to expand further, connect with new people and keep giving the high-quality service we thrive by. We feel this brand 'Instakicksz' has come a long way so far...and only bigger and better opportunities to come!

Samad Khan - www.instagram.com/instakicksz

Facebook

Bloggers spend months and sometimes years using Facebook for only one thing: posting links to their blog posts. With Facebook's algorithm changing over the years, fewer and fewer posts are shown to your followers. If all you're posting is links to your blog you'll find yourself receiving very few comments, likes and shares.

Remember that a Facebook page is an extension of your brand and not just a place to advertise your latest posts.

Instead of just promoting your latest blog post, you should be posting relevant content from other sources interspersed with your own content. If you see an article that fits really well with your blog aesthetic or is about a topic you frequently discuss then repost it or comment and share the article. You'll find this will increase your engagement and readers will start to see these posts in their feed/timeline, interact with them, and get to know your brand on a more comprehensive level.

Here's a perfect example, if you're a beauty blogger then your Facebook page should have promotions and links to your beauty blogs, beauty reviews (including videos), but it should also have content that has to do with beauty accessories, current trends in the world of makeup, or beauty as a whole.

You should also consider posting articles, photos and videos with titles such as "5 Surprising Time-Saving Makeup Tips," or "This Month's Beauty Hacks,".

See what's happening here? Your readers aren't just seeing a picture of your latest blog post. They're getting an entire experience from your Facebook page. Engagement will go up, and readers will continue to click on and see more of your future content.

Why Use Facebook

Driving traffic to your blog is essential. Regardless of the quality of articles you write, without readers, your blogging efforts are pretty pointless.

Facebook provides incredible opportunities to increase your exposure and gain new followers and readers. Facebook users spend nearly one hour per day on the social networking site. That's a lot of Facebook time. This is why every blogger – big or small – should consider advertising on Facebook. It's a great opportunity for a blogger to reach new followers, gain more likes, create a platform where customers can discuss the products and when done successfully allow readers to spread the word about your qualities.

How To Setup And Manage Facebook

Facebook, is one of many social media platforms that everyone and their mama (literally) are talking about. Nowadays, every business and blogger can be found on Facebook. So how do you make your Facebook page stand apart from the rest? How do you customise your Facebook page to suit your brand and attract more followers and brands for collaboration deals?

Read on as we make your life a little bit easier and your Facebook page a whole lot prettier.

Let's start at the top, your profile picture, people like to see real faces. Try to stay clear of using your logo as your profile photo. In some small business situations, this can work, but if you're a blogger you'll want to use a personal favourite selfie to grab readers attention.

Your cover photo should also represent your brand with the same colour scheme and vibe used on your website. Your profile photo (which should be the same across all of your social media networks) and your cover photo are the first impressions of your Facebook page.

Keep your "about" section short and sweet. This section used to be displayed at the top of the page, but now your followers must click through to read it. There are options for a short summary and a long summary to add more details.

Facebook Tips

Engage With Your Followers

Facebook has a hierarchy of interaction as part of their latest algorithm updates. Likes are the least rewarded. If someone likes your post, awesome for you, but your reach won't go up significantly. Shares are second best for increasing your reach, and comments are the absolute best! The more people that comment on your post, the more people will see your post. Try asking an engaging question to encourage people to comment on your post, we find giveaways or competitions also work well for comments.

Other ways to engage with your followers include;

Become personal friends with your followers. Lots and lots of bloggers are sending personal friend requests to their readers now. Why? You are way more likely to see what a friend posted than what a fan page posted. Bloggers are capitalising on that opportunity by becoming Facebook friends with their readers and then posting their blog links to their personal page. Some really big bloggers have started setting up a second personal account to take advantage of this Facebook trick.

Post videos! One of the latest algorithm updates gives slightly more preference to videos.

Don't sound like a salesperson when you do product reviews and brand collaborations. Less preference is given to posts that sound overly promotional.

Do not use a lot of salesperson phrases such as, "Click now! Comment and share! Sale ends tonight! Don't miss out!

Some of our tips will be eye-openers, and some may seem too fundamental to capture your attention. Trust us on this, though: It's the fundamentals that will keep you afloat when others flounder.

For best results, you may want to work through our tips as a checklist. First, read through to see which tips you are already implementing. Then come back through, one by one to put the elements you're missing altogether into practice.

Build A Facebook Newsletter.

While Facebook is an extremely useful and powerful social media platform, remember that you will never truly 'own' your audience. Your communications with your Facebook followers will always be limited by algorithms and a filtered newsfeed. For this reason, it's important to make sure you're always moving your fans to your email list. One of our favourite ways to do this is to promote a valuable free e-book/blog post/offer/promotion in exchange for an email address!

Ask Questions To Boost Your Engagement.

Some bloggers are still using Facebook as a way to broadcast a one-way message to their followers. However, Facebook works best when you use it for two-way conversations. One of the best ways to do this is to use questions in your posts. Ask your audience for their thoughts and opinions, then be sure to respond to their feedback.

For example, if you're reviewing a beauty product, end the review with a question similar to 'Who else has tried this product and what's your thoughts'.

Use Buzzsumo & Google Trends.

Use free tools such as Buzzsumo and Google Trends to find the most popular content for a given subject. Plug in a relevant topic, and Buzzsumo will give you a list of the most popular content on that topic, based on the number of social shares it has received.

Save Articles With "Save for Later".

Have you tried Facebook's "Save" feature?

With more and more link posts creeping into your news feed every day, the Facebook Save feature is a great little tool to help you collect relevant content you can reuse for your Facebook page.

Saving a link on Facebook is easy. On the post you want to save, click on the arrow on the top right corner and choose "Save ...".

Monitor Other Bloggers.

Did you know you can see top posts from pages of other bloggers you watch within Facebook Insights?

This makes monitoring the content of your closest competitors extremely convenient!

To see these posts, go to Facebook Insights and then click the 'Posts' tab and then click on 'Top Posts from Pages You Watch'.

Run Competitions And Pin Them.

It is surprising how many Facebook Page owners still aren't aware of the pin feature.

Pinning a post (such as a giveaway or competition you're running) to the top of your Facebook Timeline increases post visibility.

Click on the downward-facing arrow on the top right-hand corner of the post you want to pin and hit "Pin To Top".

Consider When To Post

We bet you've heard this a million times. It's true, but there's a catch! You need to post at the best time for your Facebook Page and your audience.

Use research from outside sources as a guide, but always remember that your Page is not necessarily like others.

Continuously tweak and study to find the perfect times for posting. Remember: Those times often shift with the seasons.

Also remember that Facebook is a low volume/high-value type of social network. Don't post too frequently - followers get frustrated with too many posts.

Hashtag Blogger recommendation;

Minimum: 3 times per week.

Maximum: 10 times per week.

Always aim for quality content over quantity.

Facebook Boosting

Boost format Ads are used regularly by Facebook and Instagram advertisers. Boosting a post is the easiest and quickest type of ad you can run on Facebook. To run a boost post, simply publish a normal post on your Facebook newsfeed and then click the blue 'boost post' button and set a target audience for your advert. You then need to set a budget of say £5 and run this promotion over three days.

Below we have two different case studies to show you. The first one is a boost done by Katie Corio. You can see the difference in engagement between the the two posts

The second post is from a parenting app and blogging company LetsCoo. They have increased their boost budget slightly to improve the reach of their posts and as you can see the difference between a boosted post and an organic post can be dramatically different.

Facebook Analytics

Facebook analytics tools are a great way to measure the success of your social media campaigns. Facebook insights will give you everything you need to know about your audience and your Facebook page.

When you first access your Insights panel you are presented with an overview of the performance of your Facebook Page. From here you will see the number of Likes, reach and engagement. You will also see a snapshot of the performance of your last five posts.

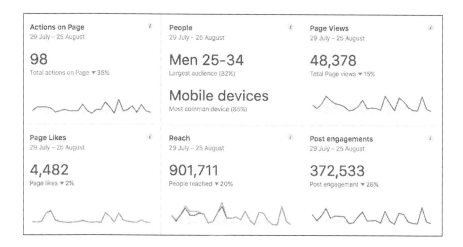

One of the most common things people want to look at it their analytics is likes and reactions that have been gained on a particular post. Insights allows you to see which posts gain the most or least engagement and gives you an idea of how you campaigns are working.

To view your likes, select it along the left hand side of the screen. From here you can set a date range and check the performance of your page over time.

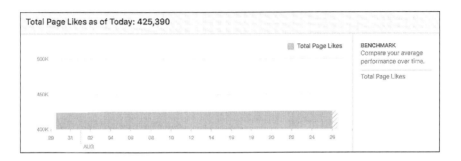

The next graph in this section is "Net Likes". Using the colours on the graph you can see the number of people who have unliked your page on certain days within the date range you have selected. From here it will give you a breakdown of where those likes have come from. Are they paid or organic?

You want to look at where you have spikes in likes and then check this against the content that was posted that same day. Can you see any patterns developing in your content delivery?

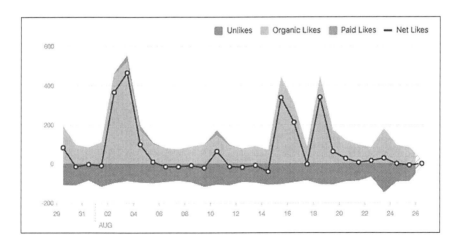

The following graph displays were the likes have occurred. This shows you if the likes came from Ads, your page, page suggestion, mobile and uncategorized.

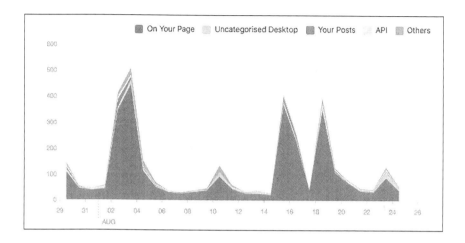

The next section of Insights we find helpful is reach. First and foremost you need to make sure you fully understand reach. It's essentially the amount of people who can view your posts at any one time. If you have 3000 followers, you have the potential to have a reach of 3000 people. Straightforward right?

Through Facebook analytics you are able to see your organic reach vs your paid reach and this will show you which posts are gaining the best views. Which content works best for your page? Is it photos? Videos? You can also see where you followers have hidden your posts or if they have reported it as spam

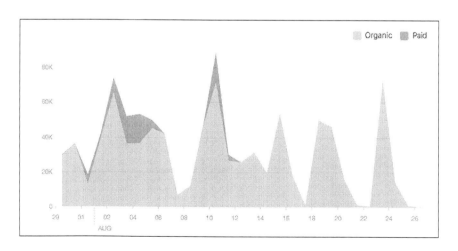

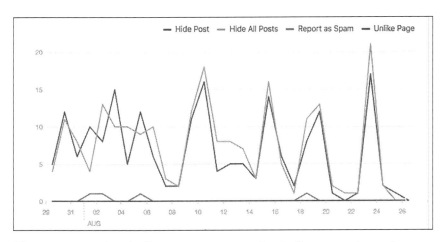

If you want to break down your posts individually so see how they are performing you may want to use the 'Posts' tab. This is broken down to three very useful categories. When Your Fans Are Online, Post Types and Top Posts.

When Your Fans Are Online help you figure out based on data from one week the best times for you to post.

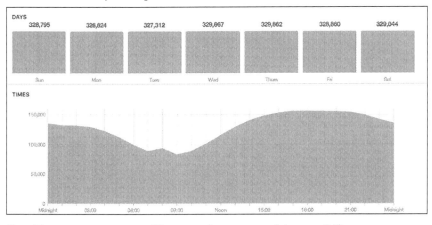

Post Types is a great way of learning how successful your different posts ares. If you have shared videos, photos or a link you will see the average reach the engagement.

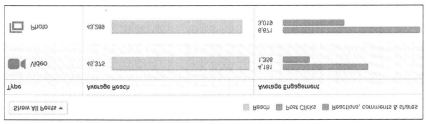

Top posts from pages you watch is fantastic way to check out what your competitors are doing. What are they doing that works for them? Are you doing something similar?

The final tab we recommend you using is the 'People' tab. From here you are able to break down the demographics of your audience. You are able to see which content they like most, what they don't like meaning any posts they might hide or ignore. It will also show you when they are online most. As a blogger understanding your audience is vital and you should spend some time digesting this data.

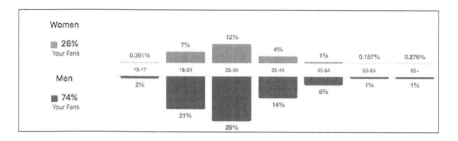

Country	Your Fans	City	Your Fans	Language	Your Fans
United States of America	124,791	Mexico City, Distrito Fed...	10,566	English (US)	199,558
Mexico	39,052	Tehran, Tehran Province	6,729	Spanish	58,358
India	20,637	New York, New York	2,901	English (UK)	27,138
Brazil	19,939	Cairo, Cairo Governorate	2,861	Portuguese (Brazil)	19,554
Iran	14,511	New Delhi, Delhi	2,855	Spanish (Spain)	18,956
United Kingdom	12,617	Melbourne, Victoria	2,349	French (France)	15,022
Australia	11,398	London, England	2,275	German	8,590
Canada	9,014	Rio de Janeiro, Rio de J...	2,010	Italian	8,550
Italy	8,779	Houston, Texas	2,005	Arabic	7,976
Germany	7,954	Los Angeles, California	1,941	Polish	6,119

Twitter

Still known as one of the most used social media platforms within the business world, the short message communication tool allows you to send and receive tweets of up to 140 characters long.

The significant push towards both social media and branding has made it nearly impossible to avoid using Twitter for your business. Whether you're educating customers about your product or service, reaching a new audience or promoting your brand, Twitter is one of the most useful places to be to achieve your marketing goals.

How To Setup And Manage Twitter

To ensure you get off to the good start, here are some easy-to-follow tips on how to optimise a Twitter account for your business.

Choosing Your Twitter Username

Nothing expresses your brand on Twitter more than your profile username. This name appears next to all of your tweets, and is how people identify you on Twitter. When deciding a name for your Twitter account, avoid using punctuations to keep your name easy to type on mobile devices.

Profile Images

Twitter has two different types of images that will represent your blog. It's important that you take advantage of using both image sets and upload eye catching images. Your main profile picture is a typical square photo that appears next to all the tweets you send out.

Build A Strong Profile

It's very important that you complete your Twitter profile settings to help gain maximum exposure. In the profile settings tab you will find the following:

Location Settings

This feature enables you to tell people where you're based.

Website Details

You'll want to share your web address with your followers.

Bio

You get up to 160 characters to tell people what your blog is about and what you have to offer. Make it short and snappy but clear and precise.

Twitter Tips

For those of you who already have a Twitter account let's share some useful tips on increasing your Twitter followers.

Unless you're a celebrity like Justin Bieber or Kim Kardashian, you're going to have to work hard on building your initial following on Twitter. To do this, you'll want to see a month or two to make Twitter you're primarily social media account and double up on your posts and tweets.

It's not just about what you can provide and what you would like to talk about when it comes to Twitter. It's worth having a look at what your community/ fans are talking about. You can do this by using the search feature on Twitter or even by looking on popular blog sites for related news.

Once you have something to talk about, join in the conversation and try to help others online.

For example, if you are a fashion blogger and you see #Oscars trending, you can join in the conversation as a fashion expert and talk about the eye-popping moments as celebrities walk the red carpet.

A common mistake on Twitter, is not using images alongside your blog posts. It makes the posts far more engaging and your followers are more likely to click it. Think about it, if you're scrolling down your Twitter feed, what are you more likely to click on? A text based tweet? Or a picture of some amazing looking food? Try it, you will wield improved results almost instantly. However, don't go overboard with it. It's always good to mix things up so you are offering your readers something different. But you a mix of text, links, video and photo updates to add some variety to your posts.

Having a schedule for you Twitter posts is certainly something you should consider. Once you have figured out the best times to posts you're going to see a big impact on the traffic you send to your blog by then following this schedule. One huge advantage of scheduling your tweets in advance is that you're not having to be on your phone or computer all day every day. You can have the confidence that your blog is still getting out there and your Twitter feed is still active

Use timesaving tools and schedule your Tweets - There's lots of free tools that you can use to schedule your Tweets. This is a fantastic way to spend a weekend to set up the following week's content for Twitter and set times that best engage with your followers. You can find a list of free Twitter tools atwww.heartcms.com/freetools.

Analytical data shows that the more you Tweet, the more followers you're likely to gain. If you're Twitter account is fairly new or hasn't been very active, this is probably the best time to dedicate yourself to Twitter. Your initial immersion will pay off in terms of "market research," as well: you'll sharpen your brand's voice, get comfortable with the medium and its quirks such as hashtags, @ replies, and learn the types of content that appeal to and engage your followers.

It's not rocket science to figure out that the more followers you have the greater our influence is. However, just having the followers isn't always enough. You need to make sure you're are engaging with the. So if you're are using Twitter alongside your blog, or you are thinking of using it. It's not enough using it to just tweet your blog posts. Why not take 5-10 minutes to look through your feed and retweet, favourite and reply to comments or possible questions your followers might have asked. This helps in two ways, you're not only increasing your engagement rate, but you're getting your account seen.

Respond to users who are interested in similar content - When you comment, retweet or even favorite a Tweet, other Twitter users will notice that your share a similar interest in content and therefore will be inclined to follow you.

Retweeting is a great way of adding further variety to your Twitter feed. You will continue to keep things interesting and you'll often find that other bloggers will reciprocate. Why not take part in a Twitter retweet thread on Facebook? These are becoming more and more popular recently

Retweet inspirational quotes - Regardless of your blog's industry, posting inspirational quotes is one of the very few methods that will guarantee you likes. Quotes tend to see higher engagement on Twitter because people enjoy reading them and retweeting them. Remember to always hashtag your #quotes.

Have you pinned a tweet yet? Then why not give this a go. Twitter allows you to pin tweet to the top of you feed. So when someone visits your profile this will be the first tweet they see. If you're looking to promote a product or a competition or a blog post that you really want your followers to read. Then pin it to the top of your profile.

Twitter chats are an awesome way of finding new people to follow and opens another channel for people to follow you too. There are loads of Twitter chats going off these days so make sure you get involved. If you're not aware of any use the search function to find some and get involved. When you're involved in a Twitter chat you're required to use a hashtag so it makes it really easy for other people to find you. So whilst these chats are happening, why not post your most recent blog post and add the Twitter chats hashtag to it.

Finally, you want to find people who have shared interest in the things you blog about. If you're a food blogger, then make sure you follow your favourite bloggers, brands and PR companies that work within that industry. This can be done in any industry, so whether you're a beauty, parenting, lifestyle, fashion blogger or whatever your industry is, this will help.

Twitter's Algorithm

Your followers will likely follow hundreds of other people on Twitter, maybe thousands, so when they open Twitter your content can be easily missed. It is therefore important to know the best timings to post by split testing and reviewing your data through analytics. With Twitter's recent updates they have shared a new timeline feature that helps their followers to catch up on the best Tweets based on people they follow, as well as past interests.

How It Works

When you open Twitter after being away for a while, the tweets you're most likely to care about will appear at the top of your timeline, still recent and in reverse chronological order. The rest of the tweets will be displayed right underneath, also in reverse chronological order, as always.

We've already seen that people who use this new feature tend to Retweet and Tweet more, creating more live commentary and conversations, which is great for everyone, especially for you as a business. If you provide your customers engaging fun content, they are not only likely to keep following you but also see your content at the top of their new feeds.

Twitter Analytics

As you've probably already picked up reading this book, data is key to success. So make sure you are using Twitter analytics to help you refine everything you do.

Twitter analytics is open to anyone who uses Twitter. So if you're a brand, blogger or company you get full access to their analytics.

Visit **analytics.twitter.com**

There's a number of useful tools that Twitter analytics gives you and we are going to take your through some of our favourites.

As a blogger it's important that you have an understanding of the interests of your followers. We are going to use the example of a parenting blogger here. When you delve into this section of analytics you want to see their interests are wholly aligned with your industry. As you can see from the graph below, for a parenting blogger the interests of their followers totally matches their industry and these are the types of peop

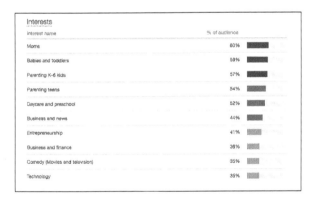

I.e. they want engaging in their content.

We've spoke about tweeting at the right times and setting up a schedule. One piece of data that feeds directly into this is the geographical location of your followers. Your morning may well be someone else's night. You'll find this under the demographics tab.

Country	
Country name	% of audience
United Kingdom	68%
United States	15%
Canada	3%
France	2%
Spain	1%
India	1%
Australia	1%
Italy	< 1%
Austria	< 1%
Ireland	< 1%

Each tweet is broken down for you and it's the engagement rate you want to be looking at. This will help you figure out which posts yo ur followers engage with most.

If a user clicks on any of the following Twitter counts it as engagement:

Impressions	Engagements	Engagement rate
88	3	3.4%
81	0	0.0%
66	1	1.5%

- Retweets
- Links
- Replies
- Cards
- Follows

- Hashtags
- Favorites
- Embedded media
- Username
- Profile photo
- Tweet expansion

Periscope

A live streaming video mobile app purchased by Twitter in February of 2015, has been the talk of the town since its official launch on March 26, 2015. Periscope lets you talk in front of a live audience and engage with viewers from around the world. Think YouTube but live, think Snapchat but longer.

Periscope enables you to "go live" via your mobile device anytime and anywhere. The app enables you to become your own "on the go" broadcasting station, streaming video and audio to any viewers who join your broadcast. Periscope is an app that truly takes advantage of its mobile platform incorporating notifications and location as well as social sharing (on Twitter of course), live discussions and feedback.

Once a broadcast is over, your followers can watch a replay, and also provide feedback, within Periscope for up to 24 hours. After that, the broadcast is removed from the app. Never fear however, each of your broadcasts can be saved to your mobile device and, once you've got it there, it can be published and shared online just like any other video.

Why Use Periscope

There are a number of reasons you should be using Periscope for your brand;

Product Demonstrations

Live streaming of product demos or product reviews is an extraordinarily effective method for boosting conversions (for either your own brand or products you've been sent to review). Many business use product reviews on platforms such as Periscope and Youtube to boost conversions.

This allows your followers to save the videos and view them later on their own. This makes Periscope a great tool for product reviews, considering that your followers may want to refer back to your videos several times to see your product in action before making a buying decision.

Share Customer Feedback Customer

Feedback is becoming very important for business branding needs. According to research, 79% of customers trust online reviews as much as personal recommendations. Online reviews are unquestionably a powerful way to make a good impression to your customers, but reviews delivered over Periscope can be even more effective.

Brands can engage with customers over live video streaming and ask them for feedback on the company's products and services. Then, businesses can share their feedback with other viewers, clearly demonstrating the support they have for them.

Reviews that are made over live video come across as much more genuine than text reviews published on a webpage, which is why we expect to see many brands using Periscope to solicit customer feedback in the near future.

Be The First

Be the first to share breaking news in your industry. Keeping customers and fellow blogger updated about recent developments is very important.

You'll be setting yourself or your brand as an authority figure and gain more followers and views.

Hosting Interviews & Takeovers

Conducting interviews and organising takeovers is a great way to improve your brand image, customers will look more favorably on your brand if you're actively engaging with other experts in your field.

It's worth e-mailing and messaging other bloggers and brands to work with. This will benefit both parties involved as you will gain from their followers and they will gain from your audience.

Run Q&A Sessions

More brands and bloggers are using online Q&A sessions to communicate their messages with customers than ever before, as they're a great way to clarify any points of confusion and de-emphasize any misconceptions that may be negatively weighing on your brand.

We've found running Q&A's on both YouTube and Periscope results in high engagement as your followers will want to ask you personal questions they will not be able to find on the internet.

How To Setup And Manage Periscope

The first step in using Periscope is to download it to your iOS or Android device. The first time you launch the app, you'll be asked to sign in.

You can sign in using your Twitter account (which is recommended) or you can use your phone number. If you want to easily make the most of the social aspect of Periscope, using Twitter to signup is recommended. If you have more than one Twitter handle, you can add the additional ones using the "Add Account" function under the Twitter settings on your device.

Watching A Live Stream

To watch a live broadcast on Periscope, head over to either the list or map version of the global broadcast tab and touch an existing event that interests you.

If your notifications are turned on, you'll also learn about a live broadcast when:

- Someone you're following on Periscope starts one;
- Somebody you follow on Periscope shares another person's live broadcast;
- Someone you follow invites you to a private broadcast; or
- When someone you follow on Twitter broadcasts live for the first time.

Streaming A Broadcast

When you first visit the broadcast screen, you'll see the following popup:

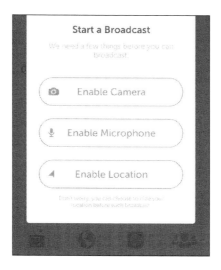

First, enable all three options as the first two are necessary for video and audio and the third can be shut off for individual broadcasts.

Next you'll be taken to the broadcast setup screen.

Look through this screen one step at a time:

1. This is where you name your broadcast.
2. Touching here toggles the location setting. If you want to keep your location private, turn this off.
3. Touching here turns your public broadcast (by default) into a private one. You can only invite people who follow you and you have to select each one individually. This is great for small classes or groups of folks you're coaching.
4. Touching here toggles the folks who can chat during the broadcast. If it's off, every viewer can chat. If it's on, only those who follow you can chat.
5. Touching here sends an update via Twitter so your followers know you're starting a broadcast. This is useful for getting the attention of those who follow you on Twitter but not yet on Periscope.

From there, it's just like watching a broadcast except you're the one on the screen!

One important tip: if you need to change which camera your mobile device is using (if you've enabled comments, you really want to be watching the screen during a broadcast), double tap the screen to switch.

After the broadcast, you'll be able to see analytical data on how many viewers watched your broadcast, how many commented and where they were based.

Periscope Tips

Create A Catchy Title For Your Broadcast

It just takes a few minutes, but try to come up with a title for your broadcast that draws your followers in. Either be super obvious (tell them exactly what you are going to talk about or show us) or leave a little mystery (announce you are going to reveal something or share something new on your broadcast). Either way…make them want to watch your broadcast.

Engage With Your Viewers

Part of the fun of Periscope is seeing who will turn up to watch your live stream. Even those with just a couple of hundred followers are getting up to 100 people in a scope at one time. Take a few minutes to say hi to them. Welcome them, ask where they are from, interact a little. It's like letting everyone come into the room to sit down. Announce that you will be starting soon but you are just welcoming people in – this can help people to know that you are just at the start of your broadcast, while acknowledging those that want to say hi. We find that by talking to people first you can let them know they are acknowledged and then they will understand if you don't respond to every comment while you are talking.

Don't Ask For Hearts

We love the heart feature on Periscope. Receiving them is fun and sometimes overwhelming. There's one thing that really bugs us - when bloggers or brands ask for users to click the hearts. People have become obsessed with them already and for the wrong reasons. By all means love the hearts, thank your followers for giving you hearts (as it means they love your broadcast) but …

don't beg for them or ask people to give them to you to reveal information. Running competitions for the person that hearts the most (yes, some people then sit there tapping so hard they don't even hear what you have to say!) is a fine line. Hearts shouldn't be your primary goal on Periscope! Asking for hearts is like asking for a client to like you. A client can like you a lot, but if they refer and share your social pages… that's all you really need.

Measure Engagement

One benefit of Periscope is that it allows you to directly measure the level of engagement you've achieved with your audience. Specifically, Periscope has a feature that allows viewers to send you virtual hearts in real time. The more hearts you receive, the higher they'll rise on the screen – and the higher the engagement you've achieved.

Spotify is one company that's already tested this feedback system, using Periscope to host a performance from Conor O'Brien. The app was able to determine that customers were impressed with his performance based on the number of virtual hearts the streaming concert received. This is a great method to understand how receptive your viewers are to your brand. See which Periscope sessions received the most hearts, and then use that data to optimise your brand message and future streaming activities.

Snapchat

You may already be using Snapchat, or you may be thinking, why should I use it along with all my other channels? There's a number of reasons why you should use it and we're going to run through them with you in this section of the book.

Snapchat is an awesome way of showing your followers the real you. It gives you the best possible opportunity to show you followers the real you. It's a real opportunity for you followers to get to know you on an intimate level that can't really be achieved through other social channels. Snapchat gives you the chance to just be you, authentic and genuine. Who doesn't appreciate that? There's no pressure to reach a certain number of likes or follows, it's just you a and the camera. For this reason, Snapchat is beginning to dominate social channels.

Have you been wondering whether you should be using Snapchat as a blogger? Well it looks like now is the time to get on board. There are more people sending snaps than tweeting. Snapchat now has over 150 million daily users in comparison to Twitter's measly 140 million. Snapchat for the win.

Why Use Snapchat

When Snapchat was first launched, it was designed as an opportunity for individuals to send pictures of their life to friends without them being shared across other social networks. Your content isn't always safe online, but Snapchat offered a way of sharing content that would be immediately deleted.

But then, they introduced the story element and this changed things. Allowing bloggers and public figures to use this platform. This allows you to share your images with people who follow you, not just the one's you follow back also. This now means you as a blogger have the opportunity to share some of your most personal moments with your followers. Snapchat paid campaigns are growing and growing fast. It's a whole new revenue stream for brands and paid affiliate programs.

How To Setup And Manage Snapchat

Create An Account

1. Download the app.
2. Go to the App Store or Google Play Store and download Snapchat
3. Launch Snapchat and tap "Sign Up."
4. Enter your details
5. Create a username. ...
6. Verify your phone number. ...
7. Add friends by username or from your address book.

How To Snap

If you're a seasoned Snapper you can probably skip this section, but if Snapchat is new to you, then keep reading.

Create A Story

One of the main features of Snapchat is called Stories. This feature allows you to take photo or video and add it to a personal stream. Each section of your story can last up to 10 seconds and will stay in your stream for 24 hours. Following those 24 hours, it's gone forever, so make sure you download the video or photo to your camera roll if it's something you'd like to keep. There's a thin line to tread here, because you really don't want to your story to be too long, otherwise you'll lose engagement.

Send Snaps To A Friend

When Snapchat was first released it was made to send photos from user-to-user. If you'd like to send a photo to specific person, take a photo or video, hit the arrow in the bottom of the screen, select who you want to send it to and hit send. Snapchat now has the use of lenses and filters, so you can swipe left or right to change the image, or better yet, you can use their facial recognition software to add some pretty cool features. Just active the front face camera, press and hold on your face and viola. Choose the funniest filter and send away.

Adding Friends

Adding friend on Snapchat is a fairly straightforward procedure. Active camera mode, select the Snapchat ghost at the top of your screen and hit Add Friends. From here you can add friends who are in your contact lists, nearby people or simply by username. You can also use your personal Snapcode which works in the same way as a QR code. As a blogger, you want to make sure your account is set to public

Snapchat Tips

Behind The Scenes - Give your fans a look at how your blog posts or videos are created or even a sneak peek of upcoming events. For example, if you are involved with London Fashion Week, take a few quick snaps on what is happening behind the curtain. So much of social media these days is a performance. You don't have to edit and filter everything you share. You can allow your followers to get to know you on the most intimate level and Snapchat is perfect for this.

Product reviews - Snapchat is ideal for product demos and really short review.

How to videos – Use your story to show you followers a step by step guide on how to do something. Maybe a make-up tutorial?

Coverage of events you attend - Snapchat is the perfect social platform for sharing your day out at an event in real time.

Entertainment - The way we see it, Snapchat is supposed to be silly. So go a little crazy and have some fun.

Skip Snaps

If you come across another story that's a got a lot of uploads, you can skip snaps that you don't want to view for the full 10 seconds. Whilst viewing the snap and you're holding on finger on the screen, tap the video or picture one with another finger and you'll skip to the next snap in the story.

User More Than One Filter

Recently Snapchat has added a new feature which allows you to use two filters on your snaps. To do this, pick the first filter you want to have on your snap, then hold the screen with one finger and with another finger swipe to pick the next filter you wish to apply. Not all filters can be used in combination, but you'll figure that out.

Flip The Camera

When you're on camera mode you can quickly flip between your front and back facing camera by simply double tapping the screen.

Send Camera Roll Images As Snaps

You can send existing images to your to your friends via the direct messages. Just select the person you're looking to send a snap, enter the direct message dialogue box and send away.

Always Add To Your Story

For people to be able to see your snaps, you need to be adding them to your story. As a blogger, there's a chance the people that follow you don't follow you back. Which means you need to adding your videos and photos to you story in order for people to see your posts. You can also alter your settings by allowing people who do not follow you to be able to send you snaps. Be careful with this as you have no control over what's being sent and you can't see the image unless you open it. Having images in your story also means that your followers can see your images for 24 hours, not just 10 seconds.

Delete Snaps From Your Story

If you make a mistake, you can easily remove snaps from your story. Hit the settings wheel on your snap you wish to delete and you're done.

Promote Yourself And Others Too

It's not so easy to be found on Snapchat as it is on other social media channels. It's important you promote yourself on other social media channels in order to gain followers. You can only be added by username or by being in someone's address book. It's likely your followers don't have your number, so make sure you let them know you're using Snapchat.

Snapchat takeovers are a great way to gain exposure for yourself and other bloggers. Swapping accounts for a day, or even an hour is a great way of gaining more exposure. So spread the love.

Things To Avoid

1. Ensure you check the length of your photos. Try to avoid snaps that are too short
2. Keep interested in your videos by ensuring something happens in the first half. Your followers will switch off after the first few seconds if it's not something interesting straight away.
3. If you're sharing something important add it to the caption. Lots of users may have their phones flicked on silent and may miss the main part of your Snapchat.
4. Use filters to lighten the mood, if you're a little nervous when you first start then they can be a great ice breakers. But don't overuse them. Remember, your followers follow you for you.

YouTube

With Google's recent updates they often include videos within its search result pages, and as a blogger you need to be making the most of YouTube.

Did you know that video content already makes up 64 percent of all internet traffic, according to Cisco's 2014 Visual Networking Index, and it's forecast to grow to 80 percent of all traffic by 2019. The popularity of video has spread to advertising and marketing, as well, with eMarketer estimating that $7.77 billion was spent on online video advertising in 2015.

The presence of video itself affects the most important SEO ranking factor (content). Video is evidence of quality content and helps send signals to search engines that your website contains rich media (videos) relevant to search requests. It is expected that search engines will continue to increase the ranking factor of including video as consumers demand video in search results.

Creating and optimising videos on platforms such as YouTube, Dailymotion, Viddler and Photobucket have many benefits including more exposure on the first page of Google.

Not only are well optimised videos indexed by Google but they rank completely separate from your normal organic rankings. Which means if your website is new and nowhere to be found on Google, a quick way to see rankings appear on page 1 of Google is by uploading and optimising videos.

Lots of business owners and bloggers avoid making videos because they think they are time consuming, expensive or don't really know what topic to make a video on. You can easily get promotional and explainer videos created and published for as little as £100, or you can grab a camera and a blank wall and film yourself talking about your products and services.

When optimising your videos make sure you use keyword rich descriptions, titles and mention locations if you're a company offering local services.

While shares and links to your YouTube video won't count as backlinks to your website, you can create two backlinks from a YouTube account. Create a

YouTube channel and add your website page into your channel's profile. Also insert your link in the video description.

In addition to creating videos and uploading them to video sharing websites such as YouTube, you'll want to embed these videos to your own website. Google and other search engines tend to like videos and in particular like videos that show relevant titles and descriptions to the landing pages of your website.

Once your videos are uploaded to the video sharing sites and embedded in your website, you want to get more people to like or view your video by sharing it on your social channels, this is a positive signal to search engines of the value of your content. This will increase the likelihood of your video being found and driving traffic to your site.

YouTube Tips

As mentioned above, for the best results you'll want to add your videos to as many platforms as possible including YouTube, Dailymotion, Viddler and Photobucket.

However as you're probably aware, YouTube is owned by Google, and YouTube is the world's second largest search engine, and it has the least competition for eyeballs across all social platforms. To put this in contrast, here is a few snap shots of the same search terms competing on Google and YouTube;

Question, which of the two (Google & YouTube) do you think is the easiest and quickest to get a first page ranking on? Yes you guessed it, Youtube.

You may ask… Why aren't more people creating videos to go after YouTube rankings? It's a combination of a fear of looking bad on video, the unwillingness to spend a day figuring out how to create a decent video, and wanting to hide in anonymity through a web page.

What most people don't seem to realise is that you can remain anonymous behind a slideshow or screencast, and it takes half the time to create a video as it does a blog post.

Now we've given you a perfectly good reason to start creating videos for your business, we are going to give you some killer tips that work wonders.

Target Keyword Phrases

When you're doing your keyword research try to aim for words that have a minimum of 500 monthly searches. Although YouTube is the second largest search engine, it pales in comparison to Google. Going after a lower searched long tailed phrase is usually a waste of time and resources.

Use The Keyword Phrase Directly In The Filename

When saving the filename for your video, be sure to include the keywords separated by hyphens. This filename is read by YouTube's/Google's algorithm, and it can increase your chances of ranking higher.

If you were trying to show up for the keyword phrase "Hair Salon Nottingham," then these are some good and bad examples of filenames.

Bad filename - video12324.mp4
Optimised filename - hair-salon-nottingham.mp4

Know What Types of Searches Google Automatically Uses Videos For

We all know when we're looking for a tutorial or a how to, we're normally presented with videos on Google's search results.

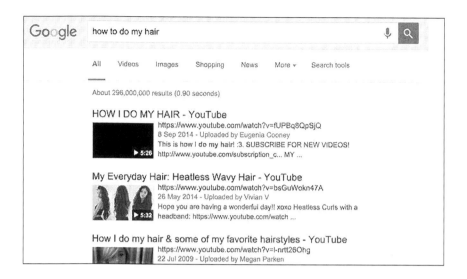

By creating videos with these keywords, you have a better chance of ranking on Google's front page in addition to YouTube.

Create a Keyword Rich Description with Over 250 Words

Your video descriptions are just as important as your titles when it comes to YouTube SEO. It is vital to make sure your description has at least 250 words and include the keyword 2-5 times.

Link to A Related Blog Post in the First 15 Words of the Description - Over 40% of people that watch the entire video will click on the link in the first part of the description. Here are three ways to double that number:

- Create Targeted Content - A big mistake most business owners make is just sending them to their home page. If your video has tips about 'how to do your hair', then create a blog post to support the video and link it in your description.
- Use an Annotation Call to Action - Create a call to action annotation within the bottom part of the video that points to the link. For example you can write, "Click the url below to see my blog post on doing your own hair."
- Ask Them to Click - At the end of each video ask them to click on the link in the description to see the great related content in your blog post.

YouTube keeps track from the moment they start watching your video and until they hit the back button. If viewers go to your blog post after they watch the video, then it increases the average time on video. This is another key factor in determining YouTube rankings. If they stay on your video page longer than the competition, then you will outrank them.

Create Eye-Catching Thumbnails To Draw In A Wider Audience

The thumbnail is the image that is displayed to people before they click on your video. In essence, it is a mini advert to draw people in. Be sure to use the most colourful and vivid shot from your video to gain the biggest audience possible.

Engage Your Audience to Increase Your Comments & Shares

Comments and shares are another key factor in the YouTube SEO algorithm. Here are the best ways to increase the number of comments on each video.

- Ask a Question at the End - Simply say something like; "How did I do?, Did you find the video useful? Please provide me some feedback in the comments below."
- Offer to Answer Questions - Most people watching your video will think you are an expert on the topic. Offer to answer any questions they have in the comments section. You can take this a step further by offering a freebie or incentive to the person that asks the best question.
- Respond to Comments With Questions - By asking your commentators questions, it can create a discussion that can lead to more comments and new clients.

Pinterest

Pinterest is a virtual pinboard where it allows you to organise and share creative images and content you upload or find on the web. You can browse boards created by other people to discover new things and get inspiration from people who share your interests.

There are currently 2.5 Billion page views per month on Pinterest with over 100 million active users. Pinterest helps people find creative ideas, that's why so many businesses, especially retailers have focused more of their marketing efforts on this platform.

Why Use Pinterest

Sizable Platform
With more than 100 million Pinners, Pinterest can help you reach your target audience when it comes to a creative and engaging brand.

Investing Time
Although you might think you don't have time, remember that pins last forever - your content doesn't have an expiry date.

Pinners Are Open To Brands
Unlike other channels, Pinners are opened to see what brands have to offer and don't mind seeing a bunch of content from the brand on their news feed as long as it is creative.

Influence Purchases
Pinners are engaged and love advocates to the channel. Pinners look for inspiration when it comes to Pinterest and save these images for when they next go shopping.

Pinners have larger shopping carts so it's something you want to think about when it comes to connecting your business to the board.

Trends
Pinterest informs you of upcoming and emerging trends and popular products. You want to think about this if you are in the fashion, beauty, home or garden industry. Pinterest display popular keywords and trending products in real time. When you use Promoted Pins, you can also track which products are in style or might be losing traction in the market. This info can help your business improve its line of products and services.

How To Setup And Manage Pinterest

Create Board Titles
When you are creating board titles you need to ensure you've got your SEO cap on. You board titles need to contain keywords and you need to be concise.

You then need to use board descriptions to include more keywords. Pinterest does not use hashtags. The last line of the description needs to contain the URL to your blog. Unfortunately the link is not clickable, however, this does give someone the opportunity to find your blog should they come across your board. Here you need to ensure the blog title and description are readable on a mobile device and follow our advice previously in the book on writing catchy headlines. You want to allow Pinterest users (Pinners) to be able to see your boards and immediately know what to expect from you.

Adding Pins to boards

Quality over quantity when it comes to boards. It's better to have less boards with more pins, than tonnes of boards with very few pines. If you don't have the time, create a board at a time. Pinterest is a social media platform and you want to look engaged and interested in the topics you are pining about. You want to have at least 10 pins to start and choose a board cover than fits the space well and looks great and make sure each board has a different cover.

Group Boards

When you first join Pinterest getting involved in a group board is a great way of getting your pins seen by more people. It's not just your followers that will see you pins, but all the followers of people that contribute to that board. You have the potential of expanding your reach here and gaining new followers. Group boards also give you another great place to pin. You don't always want to be pinning to your own boards.

The best way to find groups you would like to contribute to us to look at the accounts of Pinners you already follow. Most group boards allow Pinners who already contribute to invite new Pinners to that board. Who do you fellow bloggers pin with? Is that something you can get involved in?

Look out for instructions from the board owners as they will often tell you how you can join the board.

Pinterest Tips

If you're a brand or blogger it's very easy to manage and improve your Pinterest profile by following some of these tips.

1. Optimise board names - Unless you have more than 50,000 followers on Pinterest then it's a good idea to name your boards so they can be searched. This increased the likelihood that your board is going to come up in searches. Keep your board names short too, people are unlikely to search long names and this will result in your board being lost.

2. Organize your boards by relevance - Make sure you have the most relevant blogs at the top. Simply drag them to the to. This could be your favourite topics at the moment, or an upcoming event you are attending.

3. Link your profile to Twitter - It's always a good idea to cross promote across your social media accounts. If you want, you can turn on automatic posting for Twitter. So when you share a pin it will appear on you Twitter too. Be mindful that you might overwhelm your Twitter followers, so you have the option to turn this off too

4. Boards in the correct categories - You don't want to damage your SEO by having your beauty board being under the travel category.

5. Make a secret board - It's good fun to create a secret board you've always wanted to start but not quite sure if you want to share it right away. If it comes together and it has at least 10 pins on it, then get sharing.

6. Change a number of board covers - Keep your profile up to date and looking fresh. We recommend changing your board covers every week.

7. Delete board you don't use - If you're not regularly pinning to a board and it has less than 25 pins, then delete it.

8. Leave any group boards you're no longer a fan of - If you're not contributing to a board then leave it

Google +

So Google + has been around for a while, but most people are a little unsure whether this social media channel is really beneficial to them. So we are going to run through how to set up and optimise your Google+ social profile. Your about section can really help to show off you and your best work, gain followers and most importantly drive website traffic.

You might be asking yourself, 'What's different about Google+?'. Well, instead of sharing the standard social posts of your food or your pet, you're going to use it to share you blog posts, YouTube videos and all your top content.

We strongly recommend you take a professional approach to your Google+ account. Instead of being more personal like your Facebook profile. You want to advertise you and your best work.

The best part of Google+ is the massive advantages to SEO. Google own it, so of course they are going to favour those that use their social media channel. So follow the steps below to make a killer profile.

How To Setup And Manage Google +

Name - Even though we recommend taking a business like approach to your Google+ profile, Google does want you to use your name on Google+. You do risk your account being suspended if you use a business name.

Custom URL - As we've mentioned, there are many SEO advantages to using Google+ and the first one you need to ensure you get right is the use of the custom URL as this is will help people who are searching for you online. So your custom URL will look something like: **https://plus.google. com/+YourNameHere .** This is where it becomes a real shame that you can't use your business name on Google+, however, this does make it more appealing than a bunch of random characters.

Cover photo - Cover photos have become standard part of all social media channels these days. So it's important you use something that fits you and your brand. In the interest of being consistent, we recommend using the same branding/colours you have on your website.

Recommended size: 1080 × 608 pixels.

Minimum size: 480 × 270 pixels.

Maximum size: 2120 × 1192 pixels.

Tagline - You want to keep this short and sweet, however, you want to use your newly found SEO skills here. Try and incorporate some keywords into your tagline.

Introduction - When writing your introduction, you want to write this again with your SEO cap on. Write this in the same way you would write your 'About Me' section of your website. Give a little bit of information about yourself, but you want to highlight how you can help others and what you can do for them. Use lists and bullets points to make the content skimmable and easier to read.

Here's a great little tip for you! Where you place hyperlinks throughout your entire Google+ page, these links are automatically "NoFollow" links. Meaning, that you won't get a Google approved backlink from these sections. However, the introduction links are DoFollow. So make sure you include the link and get that backlink to your site.

Introduction Checklist
Make sure you include:

- ❑ Your Blog what it's about
- ❑ Topics you cover
- ❑ Your top blog posts
- ❑ What circles you'd like to be part of and who you'd like to connect with

Google + Tips

1. Use headlines on updates - When you are sharing something on Google+ you want to add a bold heading to make sure it stands out. Google also includes your headline into the title tag of the post and this is great for SEO and this will appear in the Google search results. If you want to add a headline you need to use * at the start and end of you headline. For example, *How to use Google+*. When you hit publish this phrase will be in bold.

2. Use images - Make sure you're using images to add a visual appeal to your page to engage your followers. If you're pasting a URL, Google+ will use an image from that link or you can use your own.

3. Use hashtags - Google+ has an awesome hashtag system that is very powerful and works in a different way to Twitter and Facebook. When you post an update on your Google+ profile it will automatically assign a hashtag or you can assign your own. You can then hover over the hashtag to reveal some related hashtags that are created by Google+. When a user clicks on a hashtag, the explore dialog box appears and will show them related content. So assigning relevant hashtags to your post is a great way of driving traffic to your posts.

4. Targeted sharing - When you are sharing a post you are able to notify people in specific circles when you post an update. You can just sue the default 'public' setting each time you update, but you will gain more exposure if you target specific circles or individuals.

LinkedIn

Many people may looks at Linkedin for a place for you CV and a place to look for jobs. However, it can be very beneficial to bloggers. You might be thinking, why do I need Linkedin as well as Facebook, Instagram, Snapchat etc. The great thing is, Linkedin does not require the same amount of time to maintain as your other channels.

Why Use LinkedIn

One thing that many people don't consider is how highly Linkedin ranks on search engines. You're only going to increase your exposure and chances of being picked up by brands and other influencers. One of the biggest advantages of being on Linkedin is this is where all of the big decision makers will be. Including where to spend advertising money. For you as a blogger, that could be your route into becoming a paid blogger, rather than doing it for free. Linkedin gives you a great chance to build a network of powerful influencers in your blogging industry. Whether you fashion, beauty, lifestyle or mummy blogger, there's an opportunity for everyone. Use this network to strike up discussions and find guest blogging opportunities.

Make sure you build your professional profile on Linkedin. This is your opportunity to sell yourself and let everyone know you're a blogger. Brands and other bloggers will look to find other bloggers through this channel. When building your profile, we recommend you use a good headshot of yourself. Not your logo. Brands and other bloggers will want you for being you. So they will want to see you on you profile page. It's really important you include the link to your website in your profile. You want to make it as easy as possible for people to find your site and see what you do. You can take this further by showing the name of your blog. Hit other from the drop down menu and enter your blog name.

If you've got a loyal following, it may be worth asking them to write you a review on your page. This will help build your credibility and the likelihood of brand choosing you to represent them. When you've written a new blog, it's important you share that post via Linkedin. You can do this by sharing it with your connections directly or you can post it to groups You may find it useful emailing people in your network and include a link to the post.

How To Setup And Manage LinkedIn

1. Use a professional photo - If you don't have a professional headshot or one that represents your brand well. If you don't have one, put it on your to do list and get one done. Don't forget to smile :)
2. Make your headline stand out - LinkedIn will populate your headline with your job title and current company. But you don't have to leave it this way. Use this as an opportunity to speak directly to your audience and show your individuality. Make you profile SEO friendly so drop some keywords in here. Try to keep your headline around 10 words.
3. Fill out the summary field with your biggest achievements - Use bullet points to make this section nice and easy to read. Think about your audience and why other bloggers or brands should potentially reach out and work with you. You can add media files here, so an introduction video would be awesome.
4. Add images or documents around your experience - Again you are able to add media files to this section too. So build up a wicked visual portfolio of yourself.

5. Be detailed - when filling out your profile make sure you leave all relevant details, which would include skills, education etc. Use this section to paint yourself in the most positive light.
6. Add links to your blogs and social media - Make sure you use the three URLs wisely and point your audience to what you want them to see.

LinkedIn Tips

Build your connections - Expand your connections on Linkedin by searching for people you know. You want to search for the following people:

- you work (and have worked) with
- you've gone to school with
- who are email contacts
- you know from LinkedIn groups
- who are introduced to you by your current contacts
- you've met offline at networking events
- who've connected with you on other social sites
- who are your customers
- who are your business partners

Ask for recommendations - Gaining recommendations is the way forward on Linkedin. Reach out to past colleagues, managers, other bloggers and get them to write you a recommendation.

Use status updates a few times a week - You want to be active and ensure that your face or brand is being seen within your network. The more connections you have, the more trust and confidence you develop in people and they will be more likely to click through to your blog. As always, don't go crazy and spam your network, this is only going to switch people off.

Use status updates to share industry relevant content - This will help brands, influencers and other bloggers know which industry you are working in and where your focus lies.

Blogging Tools

Grammarly

The last thing you want to do is publish a blog post or new website content with a spelling or grammar mistake. While the occasional mistake is bound to happen, consistently making errors in the content you post is only going to damage your brand's credibility. Grammarly is awesome and even picks up on mistakes that don't get detected by the standard spell checker including the misuse of a comma.

Stayfocusd

Are you someone who gets distracted easily by heading over to social media sites whilst writing your latest blog? You might be saying, but I'm a blogger I need to use social media. Well, not when you're looking at funny cat videos. This is the perfect app for you. StayFocusd is an extension that limits the amount of time you can spend on these websites. You can set time limits and once you've used that time, you can't see those pages for the rest of your working day.

Momentum

This is a really nice little extension. Momentum replaces your "new tab" homepage with an awesome new photo every day and a personalised message. You can set yourself one goal for the day and allows you to keep track of a longer to-do list. It also shows your local weather and gives you a motivational quote of the day.

Buffer

If you want to schedule your social media posts in advance there are a number of tools you can use. One we would recommend is Buffer. It's very easy to use and you can link all of your social media accounts which includes Facebook, Twitter, Instagram, Pinterest, Google+ and Linkedin.

So if you have a blogpost ready to go, you can schedule to share it across your social channels using Buffer.

Canva

One of the most important aspects of being a successful blogger is the use of images within your blogs and social media posts. A top quality image increases the chance of the post going viral and this is going to drive a large amount of traffic to your blog. Research shows that posts that use images are going to receive more visitors. It's also going to increase time on site and this will inevitably lead to more shares. So it's important you get this right.

You may not be able to splash out on a top piece of image manipulation software like Photoshop, so Canva is worth it's weight in gold. You can create featured images for your posts, infographics or just good images to going within your post.

You may have come to realise that no social media site has the same sized image. You want to be optimising your posts for each channel. The awesome thing about Canva is it has pre loaded templates with all the correct sizes for the specific social media channel you want to post on.

Tweetdeck

If you want a tool for Twitter monitoring, then Tweetdeck is the way forward. It's owned by Twitter so you can be confident it's always going to stay the best. Using Tweetdeck you are able to monitor the following:

- Your notifications
- Your mentions
- Your home screen
- Shares of your blog
- Your favourite bloggers

- Hashtags you want to be involved in

Mailchimp

Hopefully you have a newsletter/subscription sign up section on your website. Now you've built a decent about of subscribers you're going to need a tool that allows you to easily email all of them. You can now create some awesome emails to send to your subscribers using Mailchimps easy to use platform. Mailchimp is free up to 2000 email addresses and from then on you have a small fee to pay.

Depending on the location of the bulk of your subscribers, Mailchimp allows you to schedule your release of your mass email at the perfect time.

Google Keyword Planner

If you want to maximise the reach of a post that you want to be easily found by users, then you want to be using Google Keyword planner to search for the most popular keywords. If you create a post and then target a particular keyword you are going to boost the amount organic traffic.

In Google Keyword Planner you are able to add a number of keywords and Google will display the search volume and how popular that keyword is. It will also give you any related keywords which could possibly give you an idea or two for your next post.

Buzzsumo

If you have used Google Keyword Planner to research your keywords you now need to decide on some different topics and titles to blog about based around those keywords you have looked into.

Buzzsumo will allow you to find blog posts that have the most shares on social media. Just type in your top keyword and browse the different blog posts that are available.

Brand Collaborations

With the rise of social media platforms as an avenue to influence consumer purchasing decisions, influencer marketing and brand collaborations have become a trending topic that is rapidly gaining momentum.

While many bloggers want to work with brands they don't know how to incorporate a strategy to complement their other brand and outreach to sign collaborations.

Here are a few tips to get started and collaborating with brands.

Create Engaging Content

Before you can start collaborating with brands, you'll need to grow an audience and build a database of followers. Most brands look at engagement rates and not just the number of followers. If you're still working on your first few hundred followers, you can still attract brands by showing high engagement rates.

If you have an engagement rate of over 3.8% then you're doing very well for yourself and should consider yourself as collaboration ready. (We explain how to work out your engagement rate a little later).

Creating engaging content means that you also need to leave comments on your blog, Instagram, or anywhere else you've posted.

It also helps if you engage back. If a brand clicks over to your Instagram and only sees a list of automated post's, then it will look like you're not trying to engage with your audience yourself. Remember being engaged creates engagement.

With all that said, in our professional opinion and among working with over hundreds of beauty and fashion brands you'll need to have at least 5,000-

10,000 page views per month to build a reputation for brands to outreach to you. If your page views and social platforms are less than that, you'll want to work on growing your audience and producing some awesome content before trying to monetise your site.

Now you're probably still thinking 'how do I calculate my engagement rate?'. It's easy, for example, if you want to work out your engagement rate on Instagram simply log in to your account and calculate the number of engagement received in the last 6 posts.

Point chart;

1 Like = 1 point
1 Comment (not your replies) = 2 points
1 Video view = 1 point

So let's look at @htbloggers last 6 pictures on Instagram (as of 31 August 2016).

Number of followers - 18,227

Picture 1 - 2,452 likes and 16 comments = 2,484 points.
Picture 2 - 2,309 likes and 37 comments = 2,383 points.
Picture 3 - 2,268 likes and 35 comments = 2,338 points.
Picture 4 - 2,155 likes and 8 comments = 2,171 points.
Picture 5 - 8,426 views and 94 comments = 8,614 points.
Picture 6 - 38,744 views and 227 comments = 39,198 points.

Now that you have collected the data for your last 6 images, you need to calculate all the points together and then divide this by 6 to give you an average.

For example, 2,484 + 2,383 + 2,338 + 2,171 + 8,614 + 39,198 = 54,850

54,850 / 6 = 9,141.

Now calculate your average by the number of followers you have.

9,141 is what percent of 18,227 = 50.15%

As of August 31st 2016 @htblogger has an engagement rate of 50%. Now don't get carried away, Hashtag are a brand and not an individual blogger and because of the huge brand backing we have a great engagement rate.

Let's check out blogger and Hashtag Ambassador Rumena Begum's Instagram engagement rate.

Number of followers - 310,224

Picture 1 - 6,041 likes and 85 comments = 6,211 points.
Picture 2 - 36,400 views and 144 comments = 36,688 points.
Picture 3 - 12,700 likes and 84 comments = 12,868 points.
Picture 4 - 13,721 likes and 147 comments = 14,015 points.
Picture 5 - 8,400 views and 64 comments = 8,528 points.
Picture 6 - 14,413 views and 86 comments = 14,585 points.

= an engagement rate of ; 4.99%

Build A Media Kit

If you haven't already you'll want to create yourself a media kit. For those of you who don't know what a media kit is, it's a document which shares everything a potential sponsor or brand would need to know about you, your blog and your social media channels. It's essentially a CV, but for your website.

A media kit should include a number things, such as your blog's topics, statistics, collaboration options and social media engagement rates. It is essential to make a good impression and landing more (and higher paying) collaborations.

Build A Wish List

We recommend you make a list of the brands you want to work with and the products you want to review. Be realistic when making your list, you may feel inclined to want to reach out to big national brands. However, there are lots of small and start-up brands that would love the organic exposure that a feature on your blog or social media can offer. We've found that if bloggers with less than 10,000 followers reach out to these types of companies, you'll find it easier to partner with because there is less of a chain you need to fight through to find the right person to contact.

Locating Contact Information

Once you've made your wish list of brands and products you love (and that fit your blog), it's time to reach out and e-mail the brands!

Not only is it good practice to address an e-mail to a brand by finding out the contact's name it's also polite and shows the brand that you've gone out your way to do your research.

You'll find that a few brands will list their marketing manager's name on their website, so you'll need to do a little searching. The best way we've found to do this is on Twitter or Instagram DM. Send a tweet to the brand, letting them know you'd like to collaborate and ask them for the best contact name and email. You may not always get a name, but most brands will respond with, at least, an email address you can contact.

If that doesn't work and you've had no reply within 14 days, then you can try reaching out using the contact form on their site or by e-mailing them directly.

How To Script Your E-mail

Your initial e-mail is going to be crucial, remember these brands receive plenty of collaboration e-mails each day. Our advice would be to keep it short, descriptive and to the point.

Don't overload the first e-mail with paragraphs about your blog and stats about your social media channels. The idea of the initial e-mail is to introduce yourself and the facts about your audience and followers.

An introduction of yourself and your blog/blog topics.

Why you love the brand or their products.

A mention of the fact that you'd like to collaborate and why it would be a great fit.

A call to action, such as, "would you like to hear the ideas I've thought of?".

Lastly, you'll want to share your blog's media kit with them, too. I recommend uploading it as a Google Doc and linking it in your email somewhere.

Give the brand around 7-14 days to respond. If they don't, try sending them a follow-up e-mail. Most brands will respond to your initial email. If they do, and they would like to hear your ideas, then you have the opportunity to send a second email with your specific collaboration ideas and why they'd be a great fit for you and them.

We've also found arranging a phone call or even a face-to-face meeting works well and brands like bloggers who want to spend time with them. (This can also work for Snapchat and Instagram behind the scenes videos)

Keep in mind that it takes time before you find a business who is interested in collaborating with you. Try not to feel discouraged; every brand has different goals, budgets, and objectives. It's just a matter of finding the ones that are a great fit. Sending out several emails on the same day to a number of brands gives you a better chance of receiving a response.

What To Do Next?

If you like what you've read in this book, we would really appreciate a review on Amazon. It makes a big difference, and we enjoy reading them.

Also, please remember that we are here to answer any questions you might have, We would also be happy to offer our readers a free website report and a free Instagram engagement campaign, which will include a check up on everything mentioned in this book.

You are now hopefully on the right path to becoming a successful blogger. You may be thinking, "I have no idea where to start or what to do next". Then why not take advantage of our free website for bloggers offer.

As we said at the beginning of this book, to become a successful blogger it's an absolute necessity to have a blog site. There is simply no way of avoiding it and as you've most likely gathered, if it's Google friendly you are setting yourself on the right path to success. There really is no need to struggle with this part of becoming a blogger when you can use our team of experts to help get you started.

Lots of people we speak to have either had a friend design their site or had a go themselves and the results are more often than not, substandard. As we've said before, having a site on a free blogging platform like blogger will not yield the results you want or expect. Your organic traffic and comments will be far lower.

It's now time to head over to:
http://www.hashtagblogger.com/free-bloggers-website/

And claim your free Google friendly website.

A successful blog accompanies the following two traits of a blogger: One who is skilled and enjoys writing trending articles and one who is great and understands marketing. A blog with great content and a successful marketing strategy can't survive without the other. No one is going to read your blog if your content isn't strong; likewise, no one is going to read your blog if they never come across it.

Help With Social Media Management

We live in a world that is driven by social media. You can't ignore it and the potential it has to take your blog to the next level is limitless. You do not want to spend all of your time, energy and money in creating the best blog in the world, whilst neglecting your social media channels. It won't matter how good your content is, no one will see it.

We've recapped the points from this book and the importance of an effective social media campaign.

So, you have written an awesome piece of content and you really want people to see. You want to make sure your hard work doesn't go to waste. You need to utilise your social media channels in order to drive traffic to your site. It's a great way of getting your content out there.

Social media is going to connect you to bloggers just like you. They will want to hear what you have to say and see what you're up to. Use your social media channels to network and meet these like minded people. Being active on your social channels is going to help you meet these people who are likely going to be the ones championing you and helping to get your message out there.

If your blog is your business and you've begun to monetise the opportunities you are receiving then it's essential you are using your social media channels as a tool to market yourself and get noticed. You want to create a bit of a buzz around your new and potential followers, through giveaways, competition and sharing the latest news to come from you.

Rome wasn't built in a day and neither is a successful blog. You need to have patience as it takes time to build up your online presence and to position yourself in the best possible place, with brands approaching you. Being active on your social channels is going to add a sense of credibility and let people know that you know your stuff.

After all of this, you want and need PR agencies and brands to be approaching you. So being active and having a loyal following is a great way of getting noticed and making you visible to these people.

Social media is also a great way to see what other channels are doing. Are you following the top influencers in your industry and taking notice of what they are doing? Use these people as the inspiration you need to get yourself out there and get noticed.

Everyday's a school day right? We never step learning and even the top experts in your chosen field will be looking to expand their knowledge and learn new things. Keep on top of your social channels and you are placing yourself in the best place to keep up to date with the latest going ons in your industry. You also going to be constantly gaining ideas for your next blog post.

By now, I am pretty sure we have hammered home the importance of SEO. Your social media channels are going to help improve your rankings. By ensuring your social media channels are linked to your blog it adds credibility and increases the likelihood of you being noticed and contacted by brands.

So, you've got yourself a Google friendly blog and you are ready and raring to go. But no one knows your blog exists because you don't have a following. Social media is the be all and end all when it comes to being a successful blogger. The team at Hashtag Blogger can help out in a number of ways.

If you've ever wondered how certain businesses and celebrities have millions of followers on social media, you may be surprised to find out that they have an entire social media team dedicated to managing their accounts. That's because amassing a huge number of Instagram followers takes a ton of manual work. So how do small businesses, up and coming bloggers, and new brands compete? The answer is by running an Instagram engagement campaign.

We're offering our readers a 3-day free Instagram engagement campaign.

Instagram engagement campaigns are used by all the top bloggers you see trending every day. These campaigns are used to help seek the attention of brands looking for bloggers to represent their products and at times even be paid for a review.

To claim your free Instagram engagement offer visit; http://www.hashtagblogger.com/instagram-engagement-campaign/

You can also visit our website and click the offers tab to claim this offer.

Become a hashtag blogger ambassador

Ambassador Benefits

- A Guaranteed product to review every month (video and blog reviews)
- Featured exposure on Hashtag Blogger Ambassador page
- 1 blog a week will be featured on our homepage to over 10,000 other bloggers
- Instagram shoutouts to our 13,000+ active followers
- Exclusive invites to Hashtag Blogger events across the UK
- Exclusive offers sent by SMS straight to your phone
- 24/7 e-mail support on blogging, SEO, and social media

How To Become An Ambassador

- Provide us with 1 unique blog post a week to be featured on our homepage
- Add '@htblogger ambassador' to at least one of your active social profiles
- Review products received within 14 days and stick to the product review guidelines
- Use the #htblogger hashtag when posting anything related to beauty or fashion on Instagram

How To Signup

Becoming a Hashtag Blogger Ambassador is by invite only and we hand select candidates that we know can grow with our brand.

Please note, the brands we work with do have strict guidelines and if any of the above rules are broken we reserve the right to take away your ambassador status.

If you think you've got what it takes to be a Hashtag Blogger Ambassador then why not get in touch with us and find out if you're eligible. Email us at: info@hashtagblogger.com

Printed in Great Britain
by Amazon